THE DYNAMIC CORPORATE LEADER METHOD

A COUNTERINTUITIVE APPROACH TO EXCELLING IN THE CORPORATE WORLD

BRANDON DOHMAN

The Dynamic Corporate Leader Method

Edited by Catherine Anne White @catherine_anabel_white - riseuprunfree.com

Design and cover art by Kady Barnfield - @kadybarnfield - kadybarnfield.com

To my family.

Thank you for always supporting me and being the safety net that allowed me to try and fail many times over. Without those failures, the lessons in this book would not have been possible.

Contents

Opening

My Journey

I remember the day everything changed for me. The day my career really took off and the Dynamic Corporate Leader Method began to form. It was the first of many Sundays that fall where I spent full days raking leaves in my yard. Due to the large trees, the process typically takes me four to five days to complete.

This Sunday was a bit different. I chose to do something uncharacteristic that morning, queuing up a book instead of my typical music playlist. A book called *Extreme Ownership* by Jocko Willink and Leif Babin.

Turns out,

The book changed my fucking life.

In fact, I didn't end my day until I finished it. That next day I walked into work, called a meeting with my team, and we drafted a new mission with an intense timeline to reshape our work.

With this new mission and renewed sense of focus, everything changed. We hit our one-month goals within two weeks, and our three-month plans within two months. And we didn't just hit our goals. We excelled in so many ways, our Chief Digital Officer was left with nothing except the highest praise for our team, on a global scale.

It didn't end there, either. Within six months, I was promoted from my mid-level employee role to the company's Head of Product & Engineering for all of North America, a role they created specifically for me. I had the unique opportunity to run both departments, product and engineering, something no one else in the company was offered.

But how? It's the question I get most often: How did you do it? How did this happen?

This may come as a surprise, but it wasn't done through working long hours or getting an MBA or other advanced degree. I didn't go and get a certificate or push hard to outwork my peers. Those were all misconceptions I'd bought into in the past.

I did it through something unexpected and simple. I did it by changing my mindset and taking **ownership**. I realized that what got me to where I was, wasn't going to get me where I wanted to go. Through taking ownership of my actions, it helped me realize the missteps of my past.

Prior to really taking ownership, I relied on my technical skills to set me apart. Whether it was being really good at Product Management or being a really good Software Engineer in my early career, I expected being really good at my day job was the prerequisite to getting promoted. Turns out, that's only 1 component.

What if I told you that you could see similar success in your own career? What if I told you there's an opportunity for you to succeed and advance in ways you never thought possible?

I call it the **Dynamic Corporate Leader Method**, a method easily learned, repeated, and scaled to help you flourish and gain respect. A method that, when implemented, has helped countless people rapidly advance in their career, with someone even receiving a $20,000 raise within the first six months at a new job.

This book breaks down the DCLM, equipping you with the exact skills and tools you need to transform your future and create upward mobility. It blends my experience with heavily-researched, well-proven methodologies. As you put in the effort to engage, understand, and apply this method in your career, watch as things begin to shift. Notice the turning heads and positive momentum.

It's time to remove the obstacles and ceilings limiting you from going where you dream of going. It's time to unleash numerous opportunities in your career, by becoming a Dynamic Leader who can encounter problems and challenges with ease, able to adapt and progress amidst any circumstance.

It's time to take ownership of your career.

How To Use This Book

This book is broken down into three major sections:

1. Mindset

2. Working Smarter

3. Building Teams

In each of these sections, you're going to learn the core components behind the **Dynamic Corporate Leader Method**. Each of these components stands on its own when it comes to helping you advance your career. However, when you put all of the sections together, they can maximize your potential.

When you put all of the sections and their components together, you'll have something truly special. You'll have the ability to go as far in your career as you've dreamed.

Each item in this book is something you can take into the workplace or your life and work on immediately. As learned in research by David Epstein for his book *Range* (1), we learn by doing, through practice, not just in theorizing. You're not going to see the success you're after by just reading the words on these pages.

To get started, I suggest you read through the entire book first, so that you can understand the method as a whole. Once complete, come back to the mindset section and make your plan for implementation.

The way you're going to get the most out of this book is by engaging with it – taking notes along the way for the areas new to you or where you feel like you need the most work. It may take re-reading some sections and that's okay. Work through the book and make plans to implement what you learn.

Fundamentals

What is Leadership?

Before we get into the sections of this book, I'd like to cover a few fundamentals that will be important to your growth and help provide a basic foundation for this book.

First, we need to clarify the definition of the following: leader, follower, and leadership. Understanding these concepts is important for everything you're about to learn.

Leader: Someone who has followers.

Follower: A devotee of a particular person, cause, or activity.

Leadership: The process of influence, which maximizes the abilities of others, to achieve a common mission.

Was the definition for Leader what you were expecting? Probably not. I've others to define what Leader is in 100s of presentations, trainings, and 1x1 conversations, and I have yet to hear the above definition. I usually get a combination of the following:

- Has integrity
- Ability to delegate
- Good communicator
- Shows gratitude
- Has courage

My guess is you also thought of an image like this:

Boss	Leader
· Resources	· People
· Says "I"	· Says "We"
· Inspires Fear	· Earns respect
· Takes credit	· Gives credit
· Micromanages	· Delegates
· Thinks short-term	· Thinks long-term

+ by Agile Arthur

(Image source: (Image source: https://www.agile-arthur. com/blog/boss-vs-leader))

Any Google search for leaders or leadership always brings up too many images like this. I see at least one posted to LinkedIn each week.

What this image and bullet list above are actually showing is the individual's preference for what they like to see in a leader.

HOWEVER, having these characteristics doesn't just make you a leader. If you don't have followers, then who are you leading? You could be someone of the utmost integrity or says "we" (from the image above) a lot, but if you don't have followers, it doesn't matter.

Want to know a really great example of a true leader? Steve Jobs. Even after his death, Steve Jobs has MILLIONS of followers. People still reference him as the top player in his field to this day.

So what is it that made Steve Jobs a leader? His charisma? His integrity? The fact that he said "Let's go!" a lot? Or maybe his gift in generating enthusiasm? Steve definitely had some of these traits, but the traits that some followers were attracted to can definitely be unique from follower to follower.

In a survey of employees and executives (2), integrity was one of the top listed attributes of someone in a leadership position. With that being said, you'd then assume someone who has millions of followers would probably have a high level of integrity right? Including Steve Jobs.

Fun fact, Steve Jobs would buy a new car every six months just so he didn't have to register the plates (3). This allowed him some privileges that others with registered plates didn't have. For example, he could park in handicap parking spots without legal recourse, because no one knew who the car belonged to. Some would say this would cause Steve to have no integrity. Yet, he's still viewed as a leader.

So what does that mean?

It means anyone can be a leader. Characteristics don't matter.

Being a leader has nothing to do with title, prestige, age, sex, religion, race, or any characteristic you could throw at a person. It has everything to do with you being you.

Becoming who you are today is a very unique, one-of-a-kind experience. No one else on the planet has had, has, or will have the same experiences as you. No one. Because of this, you have a distinctive outlook on the world, a unique way to solve challenges, and a unique way to lead.

If you then try and pick a characteristic or two out of the hat and say "I'm a leader now," it's only going to end in failure. Why? Because we as humans are designed to smell bullshit and realize when someone isn't who they say they are.

Our brains operate the same as they did when we first started walking this earth. They are constantly scanning for threats to our survival. Those threats could be a tiger hiding in the bush or a co-worker trying to sabotage our project.

According to Paul Eckman (4), all humans have a universal and culture-specific set of facial expressions. These facial expressions are very slight, but help us discern who is a friend and who is a foe. You may not immediately recognize it, but your brain does.

So if you try and grab those characteristics out of a hat, because that's what you think you need to be a leader, you're going to hold yourself back. You need to focus on the different dynamics of your life that make you distinct. This is what will gain you followers.

A leader also does not just "gain followers" by taking a leadership position at a company. A capital L doesn't immediately qualify you as a 'Leader.'

Imagine you get hired at a NEW company in a Director role. Do you think those who report to you or elsewhere in the company will immediately want to follow you because of your flashy title? No.

Will they show some respect for your new title and position of authority? It's likely, but that respect of position is fundamentally different from being a follower.

Your aspiration should be to gain them as followers. This is how you'll be most effective in your role and best be able to make the world a better place.

Keep in mind, a boss is part of a company hierarchy, nothing more. You don't have to be a follower to your boss. You'll need to listen to them if you'd like to keep your job, but choosing them as your leader is completely optional.

To try and lump all leaders into this box of similar characteristics is unrealistic. Leadership is about capitalizing on your uniqueness, your strengths. Your uniqueness will gain you followers. Trying to be someone else or prescribe to a definition of what it means to be a leader, will not.

Job Titles Don't Make You a Leader

First, I want to make this VERY CLEAR (if I didn't in the previous chapter): titles do not correlate to leadership ability or your ability to lead. There is no direct correlation, and you must put this out of your mind if you want to advance your corporate career.

Think about it... When was the last time you had a horrible boss? Your first job out of college? Perhaps currently? Either way, did you respect him/her because of their title? Probably not.

Respect is something that requires your consent. No one can simply say, "You must respect me," because that's not how respect works. Again, this would be very similar to the left side of the image about Boss vs. Leader.

Do you need to listen to your boss? Absolutely, especially if you want to keep your job. However, throughout this book you'll learn ways to challenge the status quo and the leadership in your organization in a respectable way.

Now think about someone you do respect. Maybe they're a peer or someone below you on the corporate ladder, or perhaps it is your boss. You respect them for who they are as a person. For how they treat you, how they treat others, and how they give back to your community. In this sense, the community can be your co-workers, department, entire corporation, or possibly the community you live in. The respect is placed on what they do and how it aligns with your values, not their title.

If you think the title is a prerequisite to get respect, you're wrong. In this book I'm going to teach you to lead without the title. To accomplish more than you ever have before. In turn, it's going to land you the title you're after. But you don't need that title to get started.If you feel otherwise, that you do need the title to get stuff done, hopefully this book will convince you of the opposite.

Section 1: Mindset

In this first section, I'm going to teach you some actions you can take to better connect with other people in the workplace. These steps will equip you to quickly earn respect from others, and also connect with them on an emotional level, developing more followers. A follower being: A devotee of a particular person, cause, or activity.

These are people who are going to get behind you as a person and the Why that you support. When someone makes the transition to a follower, they become more than just co-workers. They become someone who will be by your side and ride into the proverbial battle that you fight each day.

These followers will be excited to engage with you and work with you on a daily basis. They will put in the extra effort to help move a project or mission forward. Later on, we'll talk more about how to get the most from your followers. But before we can do that, you must first be able to gain followers.

Mindset is all about flipping your perception. It changes the way you view situations and how you react to them. This is important because you're going to work with a lot of difficult people in your career. Here's the trick: Difficult people don't know they are difficult, that's just your perception of them.

To be successful in moving up the ladder in your career, you'll need to develop an ability to work with a diverse group of people. People who think differently than you, have a different background and who challenge your ideas. Having the ability to unite people with various perspectives will position you well for the promotions you're after.

Keeping the mindset that people are difficult will just hold you back, because it's a limiting mindset. Once you realize you're in control of your career, your engagements with others, you'll then be able to flourish.

If you want to have massive impact in your career, you can't do that on your own. As the proverb says:

If you want to go fast, go alone.

If you want to go far, go together.

Massive impact is measured by having substantial financial impact across your organization. For example, imagine you're a Sr. Business Analyst and your analysis of an upcoming product launch wound up proving something crucial.

This research led to the company halting the development and overall production of this new product. The work that you did saved the company millions of dollars in development cost, marketing, and employee time. *That* is massive impact.

Where on the other hand, your time could be spread too thin because you're working across multiple projects. Instead of making a discovery to stop the launch, you put little effort into your work, because you were attempting to provide impact on multiple projects. Most of your days were spent in meetings with little time left over for actual work.

Instead of stopping a product launch, your company went forward and lost millions. However, the little effort you provided on the other projects did result in a few thousand dollars of revenue gains.

That multi-million dollar save, that's massive impact. Increasing revenue by a few thousand dollars is not. We'll talk more about this in a later section, but I wanted to help you understand what I meant by massive impact.

This first section is going to prime you for going far. By teaching you to make connections with other people in a simple and repeatable way. By showing you how to earn respect from your co-workers in a repeatable way. We want to build a following so that you can utilize that following to have massive impact in the places you work.

We will first cover ownership, the most important topic of this book and probably the hardest one for everyone to master. As noted before, my life was changed by the book *Extreme Ownership*. As it notes in the title, ownership is a core component of that book. The book teaches many other topics and I highly suggest you read it, but for the **Dynamic Corporate Leader Method**, ownership is all we'll need for the moment.

After ownership, we're going to discuss empathy. While many will think this is a drawn-out, used-up buzzword, it's actually a very powerful tactic that will help you engage better with others, navigate corporate bureaucracy, and craft better negotiations. To gain followers you're going to need to connect with them on an emotional level, and empathy will be the key to making that happen.

Then comes ego. Ego is the number one killer of careers. Far too often, people argue to support their point of view without data to back it up. To this day, large projects get supported and funded purely based off of other's ego. When these projects finally come crashing down, jobs are lost and demotions are swift.

By understanding ownership and empathy, you'll be able to combat the ego of others and better navigate your job. But it's also important to recognize when your ego is holding your career back.

To end this section, we'll cover your Why statement. Going back to the definition of Follower, followers are a devotee to a particular person, cause, or activity. Your Why statement is going to be built in such a way that it connects to the emotions of potential followers. Once you make that emotional connection, gaining and keeping them as a follower becomes simpler.

Every section of this book is a method in itself. But once you combine them, you get the **Dynamic Corporate Leader Method**, a method that will set you up to accelerate your career in ways you didn't think was possible.

Chapter 1: Ownership

"Until you take ownership for your life, you will always be chasing happiness"
- Sean Stephenson

Alright, let's talk about how you can start earning respect from others. Respect from others in the corporate world all boils down to one simple thing:

Ownership.

I don't mean ownership in the sense of, "I own this project, I am responsible for seeing it completed."

I mean, "Ohh, this task didn't get completed the way I wrote it out. I must have made a mistake in the directions, and/or how I shared the directions, and/or I didn't make sure the person completing the task had the right training to complete it properly."

The inverse of ownership looks a lot like pointing fingers and complaining about that one person who failed to complete the task as you'd planned. Ownership means taking responsibility — ALL OF THE TIME. **You don't point fingers, and you don't blame other people for failures because you are always in control of the outcomes.**

"But... Brandon — They made the mistake...." No they didn't. Here is why: When you assign, delegate, or share a task with a co-worker, everything that goes wrong falls on your shoulders. At a base level, if it went wrong, it means you didn't do one or all of the following: explain the task well enough, give them the right guidance, or provide the proper tools/training necessary to complete the task.

If you start to point fingers, you immediately lose the respect of your co-workers. Regardless of who's at fault, pointing fingers makes you the bad guy/gal.

However, when you take ownership of the situation, it makes you the amazing/supportive co-worker people want to work with. People will immediately start to look up to you and respect you as a leader.

For me this change in respect happened almost instantaneously. Like most employees, you have rapport with your co-workers. Some trust you, some don't. The initial level of trust typically stems from two scenarios–

1.   You've worked on a project together

2.   You dislike and gossip about the same people

Don't feel ashamed by number two. Everyone does it and it's easy to fall in that trap. However, by doing this you're not earning the respect that you could.

For me, I definitely fell into that trap. I'd complain about co-workers and their inability to get work done for projects we worked on. Or their inability to "see it our way" and how we were trying to make the project better because we knew stuff they didn't.

The inverse was also true. They complained because we didn't "see it their way" and we were constantly a struggle to work with because their method-ologies didn't align with ours.

Just by saying to them, "I'm sorry, I was being difficult in this situation. Can we have this conversation again? I want to better understand your concerns." garnered respect. Their barriers lowered, and it gave us an opportunity to work together in ways that previously seemed impossible. But, as you'll learn in the chapter on ego, it took me getting over my ego to take ownership in that way.

Let's go over some common workplace examples to help illustrate how you can take ownership in your role. I'll cover brief scenarios across two types of roles.

Scenario 1: A Recruitment Manager asks her team to find candidates for a new Director position the company is hiring for.

Just so you're aware, companies get candidates in two ways. They post a job and people apply, but they also search LinkedIn and other places to find candidates and ask them to apply.

To kick start the search process, this Recruitment Manager emails a lengthy email (five minute read) and a four-page job description (JD) to her recruiters. In the email, she asks them to start working immediately and to see her for any questions they may have.

After two weeks, the recruiters come back with 15 candidates. Not one had the proper skills and background the manager was hoping for.

As a manager, you have two options: get upset and blame your recruiters OR take this challenge from an ownership perspective.

Rather than blame your recruiters for not doing their job well, you decide to schedule a meeting for the next morning and bring all of your recruiters together. In this meeting, you'll cover the following topics:

1. Share with the team you understand how they found the candidates they did, based on your direction

2. Why the candidates that you received aren't the quality of candidates you were looking for

3. Share a candidate that has a profile you were hoping for

4. Open a conversation to the group about your email and job description

    a. Be honest with them that this was your mistake, the email was too long, and the JD not clear

    b. Ask for advice on how you can improve for the next iteration

    c. Show them how you found the candidate you did and what criteria in the JD you are most focused on for the role

    d. Ask the team how they would prefer to receive this information in the future

From this meeting, you'll most likely have received a ton of new ideas for how your team would like to receive requests from you in the future. Your next task will be to sift through this feedback and try to improve for next time.

Understand, this won't be the only time you'll need to go through this exercise. All work will be iterative and will have openings for improvement over time.

By doing this, you've gained a deep trust with your team, by treating them as just that. A team. Had you berated them and told them what they did was incorrect, to keep trying, you wouldn't have gotten better results and some would have started to resent you.

Scenario 1a: You are a recruiter on the above team.

Your week starts with a lengthy email from your boss. You initially notice the email on your commute, scanning it quickly on your phone. You keep it in your inbox and set a reminder to read it again when at your desk.

Once at your desk, you sit down to fully digest the email. It takes about five minutes to read and has a four-page job description attached. You read it through once and jot down some questions you have about the job before diving into the job description.

After reading the job description, you still have some questions about what is expected of the candidate. Instead of messaging your boss or calling a meeting, you decide to ask other recruiters their thoughts on your questions. They supply some answers and you move forward with recruiting.

After a week, you receive an email from your boss telling you and the team the candidates submitted weren't what they were expecting. In this scenario, you have two options. Get upset at your manager for not providing good enough information or take this challenge from an ownership perspective.

With taking ownership, you'll immediately want to remedy the situation. You set up a meeting with your boss and the other recruiters to do a deep dive into why this happened.

During this meeting, you come forth with your side of the story. You share what happened with your boss and provide details on the step-by-step approach you took to finding candidates. Note that you had initial questions, but felt the other recruiters answered them, so you didn't reach out.

Once you've established the process that you took that led to the failure, you then work together to create a process to help avoid this from happening again in the future. Perhaps you share an idea with the group and see their feedback on that idea. For example, you could suggest that in the future, your boss sends the email, but then sets a meeting after sending it to allow recruiters to ask any questions they have about the role.

From there, you may suggest that rather than waiting a week to get feedback, you find 3-5 candidates that recruiters think are a good fit and then send them over to your boss for approval before finding more.

All of this exemplifies you taking ownership of the situation. You could simply point fingers and say, "No, the manager did this wrong, we're not at fault." But what's that going to get you? Nothing. It'll help protect your ego, but nothing more.

By taking ownership, you're showing your boss that you know how to take initiative and help fix situations when there are mistakes. This will get you respect and help you stand out as a leader amongst your manager and team.

Scenario 2: Your boss didn't listen to your idea to improve a process within your department and you're upset they didn't listen.

You, being the ambitious corporate employee that you are, decide to help fix a costly process in your department. You discovered a way to automate 95% of a reporting process that happens manually. Currently, each person on the team (eight of them) spends an average of five hours to help build a monthly financial report.

This process has bothered you for some time, and you finally decide to fix it.

In doing so, you create a process improvement document and test your concept on the most recent monthly report. You send the document, along with your notes to your boss.

To bring this to your boss's attention, you email her/him the document on a Friday afternoon. After sending it, you feel a sense of relief and excitement that your idea could be implemented to improve the department, bringing money savings and improved efficiency and enjoyment to people's jobs.

A week goes by... You hear nothing. You're starting to get angry and are upset your boss doesn't bring it up in your next 1x1.

Another three days go by and it's now Wednesday afternoon. Still nothing. You decide to fire off a stern email to your boss asking why he didn't read the email and respond to your proposal.

Up to now, you haven't taken ownership of the situation and the moment you click send on that email, you're really letting your ego be known. The act almost guarantees your boss won't look at it and will respect you less for taking a "tone with him/her."

Let's backtrack a step and see what you could have done better...

1. After not receiving a response to your initial email, bring up the email/proposal in your 1x1.

    a. If you don't have regular 1x1 meetings, reach out to your boss and ask to schedule one.

    b. If you start with an email and get no response, try instant message/phone call/something else to help break through the noise. Don't just assume your boss doesn't care.

2. If you don't get the response you're hoping for in the 1x1, tell your boss you feel passionate about this work and you want to best know how to present something like this to him in the future.

    a. Ask what metrics/KPIs really matter to him/her for items like this.

    b. This gives you insight into how they think and shows you how to best create your proposal.

3. Just do whatever you're proposing and ask for forgiveness.

    a. We'll talk about this in a later chapter.

This ONE simple thing will separate you from your peers immediately. In today's corporate environment, failure or mistakes are rarely tolerated. People continue to point fingers and shift blame, afraid of what may happen if they take ownership.

By taking ownership, you will be earning respect from your peers. Respect is a good initial stepping stone of gaining followers. Through respect you become trustworthy and believable. As mentioned previously, our brains are constantly looking out for dangers. Once you build trust, it's less likely for you to be identified as a threat, thus building your list of devoted followers.

Ownership also helps show humility and humbleness. Those who are able to show humility and be humble will have more success at work than those who constantly point fingers and play the blame game.

Taking ownership also allows you to fix the situation in a very timely manner. You can help control the narrative. You can help fix the issues quickly, versus pointing fingers, escalating to a manager, sitting through a few pointless meetings, and finally fixing the problem after a month or two of wasted time.

What I've shared so far may seem daunting, but it's not. It's quite simple.

Anytime you get an unexpected outcome on a project, task, process, email response, whatever, ask yourself these three simple questions–

1. How could I have better prepared for this situation?

2. What behavior could I have changed before, during, after this happened?

3. How could I have communicated better?

From this, you'll better understand how to fix your process to avoid this from happening in the future.

Not only that, but you'll be able to come forward to your team and revise whatever went wrong, getting back on track.

People will respect you for this. Not only that, but they're going to beg to work with you because you don't point fingers, talk behind their back, or berate and blame them when things go wrong. Essentially, you become one of the easiest people for them to work with.

In my life, when I look at ownership, I take it to an "extreme." This is not something you need to do, but having this mindset helps you approach each situation in a more calm and collected manner.

1. Nothing is EVER anyone else's fault. Every situation falls under my control. My actions alone affect the outcome.

2. I would rather err on the side of taking too much ownership than not enough. This allows me to:

    a. Have consistent and better control of my path and outcomes.

b. Have less stress in my life, as I'm no longer frustrated/angry at others.

These point out the reason this chapter is under the Mindset section. Taking ownership isn't a special technical talent. It's not like learning a new mathematical algorithm to help make a fancy new business decision. It truly is a mindset. It all starts with what we choose to believe about a situation.

We can choose to believe that everyone else is wrong.

Or

We can choose to believe that we hold the power to our success, and that learning from our mistakes and taking ownership is what truly unlocks all of our potential for the future. If you're not willing to adopt this mindset, the rest of this book doesn't matter. It's impossible to fully succeed in the **Dynamic Corporate Leader Method** without first mastering an ownership mindset, one that devalues finger pointing and instead values the notion of personal responsibility in all situations.

Putting This Into Action

- Start taking ownership right now. Make the mindset shift today, whether that means writing 'ownership' on a sticky and putting it on the top of your laptop/monitor/notebook so you see it daily. Make it your desktop background.

- Take ownership: Don't point fingers, don't blame other for failures. You are always in control of the outcomes.

- If something goes wrong, ask yourself these 3 simple questions

    1. How could I have better prepared for this situation?

    2. What behavior could I have changed before, during, after this happened?

    3. How could I have communicated better?

- Find your balance. When in doubt, err on the side of taking too much ownership. Overdoing it won't hurt you, but not taking enough ownership will.

Chapter 2: Empathy

"Empathy is simply listening, holding space, withholding judgment, emotionally connecting, and communicating that incredibly healing message of 'you are not alone." - Brene Brown

I'm guessing that half the people who picked up this book cringed when they read the word empathy in the table of contents. Why? Because it's one of the most overused/overhyped buzzwords of the last few years.

By me telling you that, I'm sure you're now wondering, "Why the hell is he teaching us this then?"

It's very simple. Empathy is one of the most valuable traits you can bring to work every day. As noted before, empathy is a very powerful tactic that will help you engage better with others, navigate corporate bureaucracy, and craft stronger negotiations. To gain followers, you're going to need to connect with them on an emotional level, and empathy will be the key to making that happen.

Can it be a shitty buzzword? Absolutely. Will it completely change your abilities to be successful in the corporate world? Most certainly.

To get started with empathy, we need to understand what it is first. There are two types of empathy:

Affective empathy: the sensations or feelings we get in response to others' emotions

Cognitive empathy: our ability to identify and understand other people's emotions

What we're going to be talking about is cognitive empathy. Cognitive empathy is something that can be learned, and that's what we're going to explore in this chapter.

Some people have an innate ability to pick up emotions and cues from others.

Other people don't, and that's ok. This chapter is a resource to help you learn and develop empathy. Even if you have the innate ability to read others, which may give you an advantage when competing for a promotion, you still need to learn how to fully harness this ability. And even if you can't pick up on the physical cues as well as someone else, you can still learn to ask questions that engage others on an emotional level. You can find out how they think, what worries them, where they need help, and then position yourself as a solution to their problems.

Empathy often gets confused with sympathy. To help you understand, here is the definition for Sympathy:

Sympathy: feelings of pity and sorrow for someone else's misfortune.

Take a look at the graphic below.

(Image source: Empathetic vs. Sympathetic vs Empathic by
Marko Ticak, Grammarly Blog)

I'm not suggesting we completely remove sympathy from the equation. By showing you the difference, it's merely to point out that there is a difference. Sympathy is acknowledging the issue, whereas empathy is action-oriented and purposeful in helping find a solution to a challenge.

Scenario 1: Let's imagine in your role that you are responsible for sending out a status presentation every Tuesday to the company's executive team. In this presentation, you share updates on budget, project status/deliverables, and timeline/personnel changes. Keith from accounting is responsible for getting you information on the current budget. In this scenario, Keith is a peer to you. You have a similar work level in the company.

Sadly, each Monday, Keith is late with your budget numbers. You send him an email, instant message, and leave him a voicemail as a reminder. Still, no response.

Sure enough, around 11pm Monday night you receive an email from Keith with your numbers and an apology. This is routine, Keith typically sends his budget numbers late on Mondays. This then forces you to stay up late finalizing the report or getting up early to make sure it's complete before you need to send it at noon.

To handle this tardiness, you tell Keith that being late is unacceptable. You let him know the importance of this report and the stress it puts on you each week. When he's late, it adds to that stress and causes you to miss sleep.

After a few weeks of no response from Keith on your request to be on time, you finally email his boss, telling him/her the situation and complaining about how often Keith is late. Keith's boss then goes and yells at him for being late on such an important task.

Unfortunately, this doesn't fix anything. Keith continues to be late. So your resentment of him grows...

This is where empathy comes in. It pairs EXTREMELY well with ownership.

Let's reverse time a bit, rather than berate Keith over email and through his boss, you set up time with Keith after the second time he is late with the numbers. This time you set with Keith isn't to berate him in person, but to get to know him.

You and Keith decide to get lunch and chat. Instead of talking about the report, you take time to get to know Keith as a person. You ask a lot of open-ended questions and learn about his job, his life, his family, his hobbies, etc. By the time lunch is over, you feel like you've known Keith for a long time.

How to easily have great conversations through mirroring

One great way to get to know someone is by asking open-ended questions. The simplest way of doing this is through mirroring. Mirroring is quite simple. When someone tells you something, repeat the last three words they said in the form of a question.

Here is an example between you and Keith:

> **You:** How's your day been?
>
> **Keith:** I'm a little tired today.
>
> **You:** A little tired today?
>
> **Keith:** Yes, I recently had a newborn and he's not been sleeping well.
>
> **You:** Not sleeping well?
>
> **Keith:** Yeah, it sucks. He started out sleeping fine, but lately it's like his schedule is reversed. He sleeps all day and stays up all night. My wife and I are both struggling through it. Work has been tough lately
>
> **You:** That sounds rough...Work has been tough lately?
>
> **Keith:** Yeaa...Not only am I not sleeping, we had two people quit this month and my boss has become even more of a micromanager because of it.
>
> **You:** A micromanager?

...You get the point.

By mirroring, it will allow you to engage them in conversation and learn a TON about them. Not only will you learn more about them, they will view you as a close acquaintance / friend as you are truly listening to them instead of just speaking at them.

Simply through mirroring, Keith has opened up and shared a lot of his struggles in his life / career. Now you know why Keith is late with the numbers. It's not because he doesn't care about your report, it's because he's exhausted and overworked.

By taking this route with Keith, you can now put together a better plan that works for both of you, one that takes into account the tribulations in his life. For example, you could ask Keith if the format he sends the data to you is the simplest for him. Maybe you asked him to format the data "all pretty" on a slide and send it. As you talk about this, you find out that getting the data onto a PowerPoint slide is what takes him the longest. So you suggest he send it over raw, in an Excel sheet, and you put the data into the slide.

By better understanding Keith's scenario, it gives you an opportunity to work together and solve challenges in a way you haven't before. It's very easy to just be angry with other people who aren't doing their part. But when you dig deeper, you can discover so much more. Strategic, minor tweaking becomes tremendous stepping stones towards progress and success.

By making this small compromise in how Keith sends the data, you can get your work done on time and relieve the stress and pressure from the situation. This opens up Keith's ability to focus on other areas of his job, something Keith will remember and be more open to supporting you in future engagements.

By helping Keith in this way, not only have you made his life a bit simpler, you've also made a new work friend or possibly even gained a follower, especially if no one else (even his boss), is treating Keith in a kind and empathetic way. However, this is not just a one-and-done scenario. You need to maintain conversation and engagement with Keith.

By helping and then walking away, you made the situation better, but your long term connection with Keith can be harmed. You need to continue talking and engaging with Keith. For example, reach out to him every other week and ask how things are going. Not just about his job, but about life in general. Make sure to thank him when he sends over the data you need.

By helping Keith, you're most likely going to gain a follower. Through gaining this follower, you've got someone new who is willing to support you on your mission. Today, it's just getting the report for executive leaders done, but tomorrow it could be lobbying for a larger initiative to help the company. When that day comes, Keith will be there to fully support you.

This same process should be used when working with ANYONE across your organization. Not just someone from another team, but within your team, your peers, those upwards/downwards/sideways of you. In a later chapter, we'll talk about delivering massive impact for your organization. One key way to accomplish this is through upward management. Meaning, managing expectations of your boss and getting them and others above him/her to support you on your missions (don't worry too much about your mission right now. We'll cover that when we talk about the Why statement. It's important to understand Ownership, Empathy, and Ego first).

The method used in learning about Keith can also be applied with any boss or superior. Let's imagine a different scenario:

Scenario 2: You pick up a new project from your boss and from day one, your boss micromanages you. The micromanaging is new; they never used to do this before.

After a few weeks of daily check-ins with your boss, status emails sent, frequent requests for updated status (even after you just provided status), and constant supervision from your boss – who has been attending every one of your meetings and offering unsolicited input – you start to feel annoyed. Your boss has even gone so far as to tell you that some ideas are "really" bad, that you shouldn't do it "that way."

You start to think.... "Why did they assign me this project, if they are going to step in and do all the work for me? What's the point of me even working on this?"

Rather than revolt, shut down, and start producing subpar work (often the effect micromanagers have (5)), you need to have a conversation with your boss. Do the same thing you did with Keith. Set up some time to talk and have an open ended conversation.

Through this conversation, you learn why your boss decided he/she needed to micromanage you. It could be that the project you're assigned to came down from the CEO and it's deemed a high priority project. If it doesn't go well, not only will it be bad for you, it would be bad for your boss, their boss, and the CEO. Or possibly your boss is up for a promotion and this project going well will solidify that promotion for them, giving them more financial freedom and a way to better take care of their family. So they've stepped up their involvement to ensure nothing goes wrong.

What they don't realize is the negative effects that this has on you and your ability to produce your best level of work.

However, by learning WHY your boss is acting the way they are, you can start to create a better way of working together, just like you did with Keith. You create a better environment by removing any stress/anxiety for both you and your boss.

This also works well in negotiation. Imagine that you're in a stalemate on trying to complete deliverables for a project. You can use empathy here, too. Simply start asking questions/mirroring with the person you're negotiating with. You'll quickly learn a lot of the reasons why they are lobbying for their point of view. Once you know these reasons, it gives you data to better negotiate something on your behalf.

Once you take the time to get to know someone on a personal level and create a bond with them, you'll be able to do more than you ever imagined.

You can't expect great results if you only do this when you need something. The purpose is to find ways to support and care for others, giving back more than you take. This is the part that most people miss.

Hopefully with these two scenarios, you can see how empathy and ownership coexist. You'll struggle to use empathy if you aren't willing to take ownership of the situation. When your boss started to micromanage you on the new project, it would have been easy to simply point fingers and blame them for causing you stress on the project. However, by sitting down and talking with them, you're taking ownership of the situation and realizing that more could be happening in the scenario than you're aware of.

Far too many people try to remove emotion from work. If someone isn't showing up to do their job, then they should be replaced. But it's never that simple.

Putting This Into Action

- In the conversations you have going forward, put yourself in that person's shoes. See the situation through their eyes.
- Once you better understand a situation, use that knowledge to make a better plan going forward or to negotiate a better outcome for you and your project.
- Refrain from judgment.
- Get to know people on a personal level. Use mirroring to help you easily and truly engage with your co-workers.
    - Try mirroring today/tonight. Test it out at dinner or your next conversation with your friend. It's going to seem weird to you, but they won't even notice.
    - People enjoy talking about themselves. Your prompts will help them continue to do that.

Chapter 3: Ego

"When personal agenda becomes more important than the team and the overarching mission's success, performance suffers and failure ensues."
- Jocko Willink

Now that we have a good understanding of how to take ownership and how to use empathy to create relationships at work, we need to factor in ego.

What is ego? Here is the dictionary definition:

Ego: A person's sense of self-esteem or self-importance (6)

When you read that, did it feel right? Did it feel like the way in which you'd define ego? Probably not. We usually associate ego with these words:

- Conceit
- Arrogance
- Big Headedness
- Self Satisfaction
- Superiority
- Vanity

As you read those, did you picture someone(s) who had those traits? I'm sure you did. I can see you all nodding your head. Do you enjoy being around that person? Do you respect them? Probably not…

These negative ego traits are the number one destroyer of careers and career opportunities in your life. Sound extreme? Maybe a little, but it's not far off from the truth.

In the book *Egonomics*, the authors break down their research on Ego in the workplace. They talk through various aspects that directly relate to the negative words describing ego above. They describe ego as the "invisible line item on every company's profit and loss statement." (7)

This is due to the negative traits and how they affect the working environment at work. It benefits you more to recognize negative ego traits in yourself than it does to recognize it in others. Recognizing the negative traits is one thing, but putting effort into eliminating them is another. This takes ownership. It's easy to recognize and label a trait; it's a completely different activity to actively work on becoming better.

The above set of traits is what causes people to fail in their careers (amongst many other things). People with high egos fail because they don't listen, they constantly take credit, they refuse to accept mistakes, and they prioritize their status above service to others.

Fortunately, there are positives to ego as well. This positive side is simply a healthy and strong sense of self. A sense of self that realizes life's situations, conditions, and circumstances in relation to their lives. Here is a list of words that could be used to describe positive traits of ego:

- Humble
- Gracious
- Ambitious
- Respectful
- Competitive

To help improve your self-esteem and self-importance, ego pushes you to be competitive. That drive and determination are what pushed you to buy this book. It's that competitive spirit that compels you to want to improve, achieve, and advance in your career. A prideful, arrogant spirit is what will destroy possibilities and opportunities.

Poor technical skills or mental toughness aren't what hold people back, it's the actions people take with their egos that invoke failure. Learning how to navigate your ego and the egos of others is what will help you succeed.

Think about one of your most recent arguments at work. When you were arguing, were you arguing data and facts? Or were you arguing to protect your ego? When you argue to protect your ego, you're arguing to help maintain your self-esteem by not being wrong, regardless of the facts presented against your case.

Success and humility go hand in hand. Progress happens when you have open conversations, when you use empathy to understand others' viewpoints rather than just arguing behind your ego and pushing other people down when they don't agree with you.

When bad ego traits take over, it's pretty evident. That person can't take criticism well, they don't want to change because they think they know best, and any idea that comes from them is *by far* the best idea. This holds back any potential for growth, because they refuse to learn from the wisdom and insight from diverse perspectives. Sadly, these same people rarely take ownership, and tend to treat others more like pawns than humans, used and manipulated for their own advantage.

How many times have you come across someone in the organization that sounds like this: "My way is the best way and this is how we're going to do it?" And then, when their way doesn't work, their tune changes to something like, "This whole thing is broken. You didn't give me what I needed to make this work. You didn't do your part. My idea is still good. You failed, not me."

This type of person is unrelenting. They have the desire to succeed and achieve, but they don't keep those in check with the negative ego traits mentioned above. Most of their time is spent pointing fingers at people above, below, and all around them.

We can learn to identify and weed out people like this, which we'll discuss later. Using data and observation to make decisions will help quiet those who are pushing solely for their ideas without any data to back them up.

To be successful in any environment, you need to understand the positive and negative traits of your ego, and recognize when to put your ego aside to get stuff done. To gain self awareness around your ego, you'll need to use the three questions we learned in the chapter on ownership. These questions will help highlight where you made decisions based on your opinion, where you shut others out, and where you weren't being humble.

Being humble is the best way to handle your ego. Here are a few basic actions you can take to strive towards humility.

- Accept ownership when things go wrong.

- Understand there could be a better way.

- Stay open to alternatives. If your mind is closed, you will fail.

- Build ideas from those around you. You won't always have the best ideas.

Being humble makes you a great team asset. People will want to open up and have conversations with you, knowing you won't argue incessantly for your opinions. This allows you to create inclusiveness within the team, thus exciting more people to work with you, people who you're likely to turn into followers.

A lot of times ego and ownership will go hand in hand. By taming both you'll put yourself in a position to succeed in ways that others won't.

In the corporate world, there are three directions in which things can flow–

- **Upward:** Your boss, their boss, all the way to the CEO
- **Downward:** Your reports or those with a lower seniority
- **Sideways:** Your peers or people with the same seniority as you.

Let's go through a few scenarios of how ego can get in the way of these three items. I'm going to share some experiences from my career to help illustrate. First up, upward.

Throughout most of my career, I've worked in some capacity as a Product Manager. A Product Manager is often described as a "mini-CEO" of a product or product feature. You get to decide what gets built, what doesn't get built, when it gets built, go to market strategies, release dates, KPIs, etc. Essentially all things from business to tech to design about a particular product.

Scenario 1: In my role as a Product Manager, I've always felt it extremely necessary to talk to users/customers to get feedback (more about why this is important in the chapter on Agile). When talking to customers to get feedback, it's customary to offer them a stipend of some sort. Usually this stipend is anywhere from $50-$200+/hour.

Shortly after the project got started, I sent my boss an email asking him permission to buy gift cards for some users I wanted to interview. I was going to interview five users and pay them each $50, so $250 in total. The company I worked at was a large corporation and made billions of dollars in revenue each year.

I never heard back, so I emailed my boss again. I sent him a few instant messages and left him a voicemail. Over the course of two weeks, he didn't respond to my request. During this time, our opportunity to talk to users was missed because of other project deadlines so we went forward with a build with no user feedback. Without the incentive, we couldn't find customers to talk with.

I was pissed. I did my job. I followed the proper reporting structure, it was HE who didn't hold his end of the corporate structure.

In just writing that story out, I'm frustrated with myself. Not only did I not take ownership, I let my ego get in the way and I failed to do things that were important to managing upwards. I felt that just because I did my job, they would do theirs. That's not always the case. Here is what I failed to do because my ego kept me from seeing the situation properly–

- I failed to educate my boss on the importance of the task. He may or may not have been aware of the need for interviewing users. He's managing multiple product managers and my one request could have come off as small to him. So he put it on the bottom of the stack.

- I failed to explain to him what was needed to execute these tasks properly. Maybe I did this in the email, but email wasn't the best way to communicate. I should have gotten time on his schedule and shared with him the request face to face. It would have taken five minutes, but I instead hid behind technology.

- I didn't influence his decision. Meaning, I was not persuasive enough to help move him from a "Why should I care about this?" to a "Yes."

Scenario 2: This type of situation can also go the other way. Down the line. Let's say that I was the boss in this scenario and someone sent me emails to try and get permission to spend a little money. If my team fails, I don't get the right to berate them and tell them they were horrible just to keep my ego flying high.

Here's how it should happen from the scenario as the boss–

- The team failed because I didn't give them what they needed. It's not on them to ask properly, but for me to ask the right questions so that I understand and can then best give them support.

- The team failed because I did not give the proper guidance on how to engage with me on requisition permission on important tasks.

- The team did not get proper training for how to make budget requests. Ex: I could have put a policy in place as the boss stating there is no need for special permission for any requests under $500. I could have placed trust in my team to use the company's money wisely and to do the right thing.

- The team failed because I didn't explain the mission well enough.

Scenario 3: This situation could also have been handled from a peer-to-peer perspective as well. If my boss wasn't responding, I could have reached out to my peers on the project to request use of their budget for these cards. However, I let my ego get in the way of doing this.

"I did my job. I help up my end of the corporate hierarchy, why can't my boss do the same?" My ego spoke for me, and it closed the door on the possibility of alternate solutions. I wasn't being humble and I wasn't looking to seek advice from others around me.

It's easy to see where ownership and ego blur. However, they absolutely go hand in hand, but are separate items. Taking ownership can be hard if you don't get your ego out of the way. It's important to understand both so that you can recognize when your ego is preventing you from properly taking ownership and stopping your career from moving forward.

No one person has it all figured out. It's important to be able to work with others and build up teams. That's what we learned in the lesson on empathy. The higher up you go in an organization, the more important this becomes. Being able to get over your ego, ask for help, and take ownership will separate you from so many others in your organization.

For example, let's look at Bryan's scenario. Bryan is a **Dynamic Corporate Leader Method** practitioner and has engaged with me through my coaching program. He understands ego better than most. He was recently put into a situation where he worked to bring digital distribution to a large corporation. Digital distribution is the selling of goods online that can be downloaded (digital distribution is how you got this e-book). Previously, this corporation had sold nothing online. They only sold through on-the-ground sales reps.

In this project, Bryan worked with two very demanding VPs who "think they know better" than everyone else who was hired to introduce digital distribution to the corporation he works at. The VPs often say they are playing devil's advocate, when in reality they are trying to protect their ego and position at the company.

Prior to Bryan taking over on this project, the VPs worked directly with Bryan's boss, a Director. Bryan's boss consistently pointed fingers and argued with the VPs, often saying things like: *Why did you hire this team if you aren't going to listen to us? What is the point in arguing all the time? If we can't do our job with you, let us work on something else!*

In one of the meetings, things started going poorly and conversation grew heated. Both sides of the table were pointing fingers, blaming the other for not understanding their viewpoint.

Bryan quickly realized what was happening in this situation and stepped up to take over. To help remedy this situation, Bryan started asking questions and attempted to learn more about the VPs' point of view, often mirroring them to get as much out of the conversation as possible.

Doing this has allowed him to truly understand the viewpoints of the VPs. One of their biggest concerns was that the sales team would lose sales to the online channel. The VP in charge of sales was concerned he'd have to lay people off or that sales people may quit. This would reflect poorly in his yearly review as he had goals around retention and sales team output.

Bryan and the team left that meeting and designed a plan that allowed them to work within the boundaries the VPs had set, while still delivering on their digital distribution mission. They designed a compromise that allowed digital distribution to benefit sales staff, both financially and with new customers.

Had they continued to point fingers and hide behind their egos, nothing would have been accomplished. Bryan and his boss had to get over their ego and push aside any temptation to act like their knowledge and experience was more important than those above them. In doing so, they could have a conversation that ultimately ended in a better designed product.

Putting This Into Action

- Get over yourself. Right now, make this mindset shift. Write it under ownership on your sticky / wallpaper. It sounds harsh and it's also not easy to do.
- Practicing empathy and ownership will help keep your ego in check.
- Remember: ego is the number one destroyer of careers.
- Stop arguing for the sake of your ego. Doing so will make it difficult for others to work with and respect you.
  - Be humble.
    - Accept ownership when things go wrong
    - Understand there could be a better way
    - Stay open to alternatives
    - Build from those around you
- Be aware of how information flows and be ready to take ownership and tame your ego in the following directions.
  - **Upward:** your boss, their boss, all the way to the CEO
  - **Downward:** your reports or those with a lower seniority
  - **Sideways:** your peers or people with the same seniority as you

Chapter 4: Building Your Why

"Working hard for something we don't care about is called stress. Working hard for something we love is called passion." - Simon Sinek

So now that we have the foundation to connect with others and take ownership, it's time to move on to something a bit more personal: your mission or Why statement.

If you haven't read Simon Sinek's books – Start With Why (8) or Find Your Why (9) – this chapter is going to give you a crash course in the premise of Why.

In both books, Sinek talks about his Golden Circle. The Golden Circle is broken down into three components: What, How, and Why. Sinek breaks this down by talking about an organization. While each organization should have it's own Why, for the purpose of this book, it's more important that you do. And that's what we're going to develop in this chapter.

Here are the definitions –

What: Every organization on the planet knows what they do. These are the products or services they offer.

How: Some organizations know How they do it. These are the things that make them special or set them apart from their competition.

Why: Very few organizations know Why they do what they do. Why is not about making money, that's the result. Why is the purpose, cause, or belief. It's the very existence upon which your organization exists.

Here is an example using one of my favorite companies, Tesla, to better help illustrate the What, How, Why.

- **What:** Build an affordable $35,000 car (the Model Three).
- **How:** Break the mold that electric cars are slow, ugly, low range, and have an overall bad performance.

- **Why:** Accelerate the world's transition to sustainable energy and transport.

During the writing of this book, Tesla has gone through a year-long transformation that has turned it into one of the most valued companies in the world, making it's CEO, Elon Musk, the richest man in the world(10) (at least at the time of writing).

There is a strong correlation between the Why and Tesla's valuation. In comparison, companies that do not understand or freely market their Why and constantly share the What have much less revenue than those that do (8).

When you think of electric cars, you probably think of Tesla, even though there are roughly 43 electric car makers in the world. There is a certain appeal Tesla captures, one that no other company has been able to mimic. The brand loyalty with Tesla is extremely strong, and it all correlates back to their Why (11).

The aspiration that Tesla's Why offers its customers or potential customers is very high. Customers feel like they're taking part in a bigger aspirational mission, accelerating the world's transition into sustainable energy while driving an in-demand car that's a status symbol.

This aspiration is also what gets people to buy a Tesla. 95% of our purchasing decisions are subconscious (12). Buying decisions are based on subconscious urges, primarily emotion. This is why the Why statement is so powerful. Not only for brands, but for you.

When you connect with someone new and you are able to make an emotional connection with them through your Why statement, there is a higher chance they'll "buy" what you're selling. They'll be more compelled to join you on that higher mission if you are able to connect with them emotionally.

The reason I was able to gain so many followers was due to my strong Why statement. So much so, that on my last day one of the people on my team said to me, "You are {company name} to me." My Why statement was so strong, it gained followers from my team and elsewhere in the company, which translated outside of the company as well. Everyone wanted to work with us because we were clearly working towards a higher mission.

As you go and gain followers through ownership and empathy, those followers will eventually need something deeper to believe in if you expect them to follow you further on your mission. They need to feel like the leader is taking them somewhere intentionally, that there is some sort of direction. This is what you can offer your followers by developing your Why.

Like I mentioned previously, the higher up you go in an organization, the less you are worried about completing day-to-day tasks and the more concerned you are about building high performing teams. The Why statement is vital to helping create and support a high performing team. Without it, people won't have a purpose to get out of bed each morning. Just coming to work and making a widget isn't enough. Especially for the millennial generation(13).

The Why statement that you create will become your new go-to way when introducing yourself to others.

Imagine you meet someone new at work and they ask your name and what you do. Most everyone immediately replies with, "Hi, I'm Keith and I work in Accounting. I report to Susan, who is the Head of all things Accounting."

I'm sorry, excuse my French, but how fucking boring is that? You think that person is going to remember you after that introduction? No. What was memorable about being "Keith from Accounting?" Nothing. No one wants to follow Keith from Accounting after that introduction.

Let's rewind and try that introduction again.

"Hi I'm Keith. I help manage the finances so that we can provide a low-cost healthcare solution to our customers who are taking care of their aging parents."

Look at the difference. How did that second one make you feel? A lot less boring and more inspired, I hope. This new employee is going to remember Keith, because Keith is working towards a mission that is making the world a better place.

The great part about the Why statement is that there is a simplified formula to help you create your own–

I _____, **so that** _____.

If you look back at Keith's Why, it fits quite nicely.

I help manage the finances, so that we can provide a low-cost healthcare solution to our customers who are taking care of their aging parent's health.

One of the keys to creating a strong Why statement is to be open and vulnerable with what you're creating. Don't hold back on how you feel about the mission or the reason you come to work every day. Let your passion for the customer and serving their needs shine through.

Throughout the book I've talked about your mission in a few places and I left the understanding of it pretty general. To best create your Why, you'll need to have a strong understanding of what a mission is. Here is the dictionary definition:

Mission: an important assignment carried out for political, religious, or commercial purposes, typically involving travel.

Depending on where you work, you could tick off any number of the items in that definition. Possibly you work for the local government as Mayor and you have dreams of someday running for Governor (political) or you work for Apple as a Jr. Designer and you have hopes some day of working as a Creative Director (commercial).

For the purpose of this book, travel doesn't mean traveling via a train, plane, or automobile. It means traveling towards making the world a better place. To do this, you won't be able to stand still in what you do. Ex: By buying this book, you're traveling, you're working to improve your knowledge, abilities, and skill sets.

Your mission aligns with your values. When I talk of values, I speak to those principles or standards of behavior that you hold dear as a person. Something that you believe in that helps give you a sense of morality. Your values are shaped as you grow, learn, and travel (both literally and figuratively this time). The values you have are something that is unique about you.

When it comes to your mission and values, you don't want to frame your statement around what you think people in your company want to hear. This goes back to an earlier chapter where we spoke about your co-workers being able to detect bullshit. If you attempt to make a mission that is not true to who you are, they'll see right through you and won't trust you. By losing trust, you won't gain followers.

When I first wrote this book, I shared it with a few friends, colleagues and random people from LinkedIn. I wanted to get a quick gut-check on my first draft. This helped me to understand if my writing was coherent and if how I was teaching the concepts made sense.

One of the people I shared it with was Pamela. Pamela is the CFO at a non-profit that builds houses for those in need. One of the main components she took from this book was this chapter about building your Why.

After she read the book, I pestered her for some feedback. During our conversation she shared this story…

> *Pamela:* Absolutely. I felt like everything you were saying was either things I knew worked from my experience or things I felt would work. Actually, I have a perfect example of one of your chapters that I used yesterday.
>
> I was getting a new tattoo and the artist asked me what I did for a living. I said my typical, "I'm an Accountant" and received a blank stare from him. And then I remembered your book and I quickly rephrased: "I oversee the finances for {non-profit} so that we can pro-

vide affordable housing to families in our community," and instantly he was much more engaged and it opened up a great conversation.

What I love about this example is that a boring accountant (haha) was able to engage and create a unique story and conversation with a tattoo artist. Having a strong Why creates opportunity for connection across any kind of background, no matter how different. This is a clear example of how two people from two different worlds can engage in a mission and Why statement.

Imagine the power of the Why statement in your own corporation. People are all there for a similar mission. By having a strong Why, you'll be able to separate yourself from all of your coworkers who tend to introduce themselves by their Name, Title, Department, Manager.

In one of my roles, I worked for a global agricultural company. The overall mission of this company was to help farmers produce more food with less land in a safe and sustainable way.

This is a simple mission to get behind, as essentially we have two options: destroy the planet to produce enough food for everyone, or find ways to grow more food sustainably.

When hiring people on my team, that is the mission I used to get them in the door. If they weren't interested in that mission or Why, they weren't going to be interested in mine.

My Why statement was really straightforward after they understood the larger company mission.

I build amazing teams and culture, **so that** my teammates can build digital tools to help farmers safely and sustainably feed the planet.

This Why statement was a true game changer for my position at that time. It showed those looking to work with me that I was interested in giving them an awesome place to work, and not just recruiting them for another job.

The result of that was a team of 26 across multiple roles. Product Managers, Product Strategists, Product Designers, Tech Leads (Fullstack & Mobile), Frontend/Backend Engineers, Mobile Engineers and Data Scientists. Our team was brand new to the company at that time, and within a few short months we were working on the largest digital initiatives for the company in North America.

While running this team, I received amazing references, such as:

"Brandon is a true Leader if there's ever been one. He's been an example of true leadership, authenticity, and courage for our entire team. Being a female developer in the male-dominated tech industry can be a very challenging task at times, and having just the right leader on your side, a leader who is supportive, extremely respectful, inspiring, encouraging, and protective when needed is more important than can be expressed, and that is exactly what Brandon was to me. He was able to put together a team of people very diverse in thinking and backgrounds yet equally smart, authentic, and passionate about their work. The team culture he helped create was (and is) the healthiest I've ever experienced — there is a lot of flexibility, people are heard, there is always a very healthy discussion around improvements that can be done and it is never just words. Things keep getting better. I will always be grateful for being able to have such an inspiring leader."

This person joined my team because of the company's Why, and the one I created for myself. I received these accolades because of everything else in this book. I took ownership, I kept my ego in check, and I used empathy throughout, creating meaningful relationships with everyone on my team. She didn't have to say the above because I was her boss. She said those things because she viewed me as a Leader.

To help develop your Why statement, look at what excites you about the company you joined. Why do you get out of bed each day and go there? I truly hope it's something more than a paycheck. What challenge are you trying to solve in your role? What problems are you looking to solve that keep you up at night?

If it's just the paycheck, not all is lost. You can easily pivot towards why you do the job that you do. Maybe you're a software engineer. Perhaps you don't enjoy the software you build for your day job, but building software can be a foundation of your Why. Ex: I build mobile apps to improve the lives of people with disabilities across the globe.

Once you create your Why statement, test it out. Feel free to share it with a few colleagues and get their feedback. You can simply ask them, "How does this statement make you feel?" Use that feedback to refine your statement.

In later chapters, we're going to learn about Agile methodology, which discusses how to test and experiment. However, don't wait until those chapters to start testing. Start asking your friends/co-workers now about your Why statement. Getting that feedback will help you in the refining process, turning it into a strong statement that others want to follow.

Putting This Into Action

- Develop your Why statement and make it a focal point of who you are and what people know you for. Implement this when you meet new people.

- Use this formula to develop your Why statement.

- I _____, **so that** _____.

- Ex: I help manage the finances, **so that** we can provide a low cost healthcare solution to our customers who are taking care of their aging parent's health.

Section 1 Checkpoint

Your mindset is an important way in which you process the world around you. This processing is what shapes your views on the world and how you handle them. If you constantly view the world and others in a negative way, your ability to grow becomes extremely hindered. The aim here is to help you build connections with your co-workers in a way that makes them feel heard, cared for, and respected. That doesn't really work with a negative mindset.

Establishing an emotional connection is an important channel through which you're going to build your followers. We as people naturally love stories and passionate people. Your unique experiences, stories, and values are going to inspire them to follow you as a leader. Building a foundation for that appreciation and inspiration require open, honest conversations, which (as we've learned) require ownership and overruling our own egos.

The four major components we learned – ownership, empathy, ego and how to build your Why – are meant to build on your strengths without changing who you are at the core.

At this point in the book you should be starting to realize where you can make improvements in your mindset. By now I'm sure you've recognized –

- Unexpected project and/or task outcomes where you didn't take ownership.
- Times you complained about a coworker without using empathy.
- Times you were sad when a coworker didn't understand your point of view or use empathy.
- Instances where you argued to protect your ego.
- Occurrences where you argued against someone's ego without using empathy to better understand them.
- A bad first impression when you bored someone to death about being an accountant...

Identifying these situations is what's going to help you move forward. You can't fix a problem unless you've identified it as a problem.

To have success, it's imperative that you put into practice what you've learned from each section. The transformation will be quick, but it doesn't come without hard work.

Sometimes, hard work requires accountability and a little extra help along the way. Whether it's discovering your Why or learning how to practice ownership. I offer a coaching program that provides one-on-one guidance into all that you've learned in this book and will help you accelerate quickly towards your career goals. If you'd like my help schedule a call to chat FIX ME

Section 2: Working Smarter

Now that we've learned the importance of mindset and the power it holds in creating an atmosphere of trust and inspiration, it's time to step into some technical components of how to work smarter. To do this, we're going to look at how your work connects to financial aspects of your company. By working smarter, you can help create revenue gains and possibly save millions of dollars for your organization. The key here is to help you stand out from those who spread themselves too thin and have minimal impact in their career.

Working smarter doesn't matter in career progression if you can't work with other people. If you can't earn respect or inspire other people, working smarter limits career advancement because you'll end up doing everything alone. No one person can outwork an entire team or department.

Being able to work well with others removes the cap on your upward progression. However, the inverse can also be true. If you don't know how to work smart, then being good at working with others won't really matter.

This is why the book is titled the **Dynamic Corporate Leader Method**. It's full of components that are teachable and repeatable. Each of these components then builds on each other, comprising the complete method. Is each component valuable on it's own? Yes. But individual items are limited in how successful they can make you.

This section covers four components. We're going to discuss again why job titles don't make you a leader. This concept is important to discuss again, because if you're not fully sold, it will hold you back.

After this, we're going to talk about how to create massive impact in your role, which is imperative if you have hopes of moving up the corporate ladder into a Director position or above. Creating this massive impact is connected to the revenue gains or cost savings you can help your company achieve.

It'll teach you how to stop spreading yourself thin by focusing on one or two major projects instead of a whole slew of them, generating millions of dollars worth of impact each year instead of a few thousand.

From there we'll move onto Agile Methodology, an important topic to read, even if you're already familiar with Agile. I'm going to cut out the fluff and bullshit and boil Agile back down to its simplest form. I'll show you how to use it for projects at work, but also how to use the methodology in your career. You'll learn the art of breaking your aspirations down into manageable chunks that will have you scaling the corporate ladder faster than ever.

Finally, we'll talk about how to properly ask for forgiveness instead of permission. This chapter is all about calculated risk-taking, moving projects forward in much faster ways.

Throughout this book, especially in this section, everything you're learning is meant to help you in your career. However, everything you're learning can ALSO be applied to teams that you run. For example, you personally want to create massive impact, but so do the teams you run. The fundamentals you learn throughout can also be applied to teams.

As we shift our focus into working smarter, it's important to continue implementing and remembering the aspects learned about mindset in Section 1. Practicing both at the same time will help you move into the positions you aspire to.

Chapter 5: Job Titles Don't Make You A Leader Part Deux

"Management is doing things right; Leadership is doing the right things."
- Peter F. Drucker

I know that we've already touched on this topic, but I want to hit it again, because we're at a point where you've learned some new skills that this notion may creep back into your mind. We need to abolish this thought from your mindset, or it will truly hold you back.

To get a task done in the corporate world you have two options:

1. A Superior tells someone to do it.
2. Someone is convinced doing the task is the right thing.

See the theme that's building? You don't need to have a particular job title to get people to do something for you. However, to get that job title you're after, you need to be good at getting people to help you do stuff.

There is a cap on how much a superior can tell someone to do before they break down and quit. Autocracy is no longer working in the corporate world. Where it exists, there is a black hole around those in power who just tell others what to do. Projects are failing, companies are getting passed up by new startups, and turnover rates are exceptional (14).

We've talked about this before, but what got you your current role isn't going to get you the next one. You need to build more skills to move into that role Not only will building these skills help you get into the next role, it's going to help you deliver more impact than you ever thought possible in your current role.

In an earlier chapter we learned the definition of Leadership: **The process of influence, which maximizes the abilities of others, to achieve a common**

mission.

Everyone in the corporation where you work is pushing towards a common mission, the Why statement we discussed earlier.

To even touch items two and three of that definition, you need to be able to influence others. Influence is NOT just for those that are below you on the ladder, but for everyone around you and above you as well.

The job title does not give you that ability to do that. It gives you an ability to tell others what to do, but it doesn't give you the ability to influence.

When you influence someone, you are convincing them that what they are doing is going to be good for both them and the corporation/mission. When you TELL someone to do something, you're not going to get the best output from them, because they may or may not be convinced what they are doing is the right thing or helpful to the corporation/mission.

When you haven't convinced someone, they'll give an effort they feel comfortable with in comparison to all the other things they are currently doing. Usually the effort they give is quite low, which means the outcome will most likely be shit and not push the company forward.

As you work through the rest of this book and your career, keep this in the forefront of your mind: you don't need an amazing title to get people to join you on a mission and do great work. But if you can convince people to do great work with you, you'll quickly progress towards that amazing title.

Putting This Into Action

- Don't let the lack of a title hold you back. Job titles don't define your ability to influence.

- Job titles don't define you as a leader. People don't respect the title, they respect the person.

- Gain trust in those you work with so that you can have an opportunity to influence them. Influence without trust is hard.

- Telling people what to do doesn't get the best result possible.

Chapter 6: Creating Massive Impact

"Never half-ass two things. Whole-ass one thing." - Ron Swanson

When most ambitious employees begin their career, they want to be a part of a lot of different projects. There are a some good of reasons for this–

1.   Great exposure.

     a.   Get to meet a lot of new people.

     b.   Discover more about the business.

     c.   Learn a lot about various functions inside the company.

2.   Opportunity to have impact in a lot of various projects.

3.   Help refine your skills.

4.   Find things you truly enjoy working on.

All of these items are good and they help you get started in your career. If you're fresh out of college and just getting started at a new company, joining many projects can be helpful. It's helpful because often the toughest part of starting a new job is learning the organization, the departments, the process, and who the shot-callers are. Learning these things can easily take two to six months, depending on the size of the organization. Learning these isn't a one-and-done process. You'll continue to grow in knowledge as your role changes and as the company changes.

It's beneficial to your career to put time and effort into learning the company/organization/departments when you get started. The easiest way to do this is being a part of multiple, diverse projects.

However, after two to three years in your career, this practice of being a part of multiple projects should come to an end. Continuing this practice will be detrimental to your career. The more projects you put time into, **the less**

impact you can have for the organization. The more projects you work on, the more hours each day/week you end up working. Long hours and success are not correlated.

In fact, this belief is one of the major components that holds you back from true success. I'm here to make the claim you need to work less than 40 hours a week, especially the higher up the ladder you go (more about that later).

But.. But... Brandon, that's how many I'm supposed to work. They tell me to be in the office 40 hours a week...

If you're a salaried worker, your company may have a "guideline" or "expectation" on the hours you need to work. Typically, it's not a rule that's set in stone, just an expectation.

If your boss is forcing you to be in the office all 40 hours and you aren't running a factory machine, you have a micromanaging boss who doesn't trust you. When someone micromanages you, it typically means there is a breakdown of trust. Meaning, your boss doesn't trust you to accomplish the tasks you were assigned.

Working less hours per week will still work for you, you just need to earn trust. Here is a quick sidebar on how to build trust with a micromanaging boss:

How to Deal With a Micromanaging Boss

How to earn trust:

- Take ownership of the situation. You need to be the one to build trust. Your boss isn't going to do this part for you.

- Get over your ego. Regardless of how great you think you are, your boss still doesn't trust you. It's on you, not them to build this trust.

- Supply them with tons and tons of data about what you're doing.

- Once you've supplied them with data, supply more because it's still not enough for them.

- Copy them on important emails about the project or project deliverables.

- Deliver impact (this chapter is about this). Giving data and status updates isn't enough, you actually have to accomplish something on the project.

- Continually deliver impact and make progress. Your relationship will take time to grow. It's not going to happen in a week. Maybe not even a month. Stick to the plan and keep pushing forward.

- Repeat the cycle and things will get better.

- Don't let your ego get in the way of improving the relationship.

Before moving forward with some of the other practices in this chapter, you need to make sure you have any trust issues cleared up. This requires you to take ownership of the situation.

Working across multiple projects doesn't give you an opportunity to have massive impact for your organization. Having massive impact is what's going to get you standing out and moving up the ladder much quicker. Why? Because the impact you have is going to be in the millions of dollars, versus just the thousands, or even worse, none at all.

To illustrate this, I want to share a scenario from my career. In the below example, I speak from the viewpoint of a manager.

In one of my roles, I worked as an Innovation Lead. My purpose was to bring new innovative digital concepts to a large agricultural corporation. To test out how well this could be done we opened an Innovation Lab, and decided to hire interns instead of full-time employees. Using interns was an interim cost saving model to best determine the efficacy of an Innovation Lab.

Using interns gave us the opportunity to hire students with expertise in things like Artificial Intelligence, Natural Language Processing (NLP), and general engineering.

When I opened the innovation lab, the company gave me free rein to experiment on a lot of different ideas. The initial plan was simple. Hire ten interns, take on a few projects, and see what's possible. I did the exact opposite. I took requested projects from the company, started some of my own, and hired 20 interns instead of ten.

I did this because I felt that the more projects my team worked on, the bigger impact we could have. However, all projects are not created equally...

One of the projects I kicked off was a Slack (instant messaging platform – www. slack.com) NLP bot. This bot would allow interns to manage their schedule by talking to a bot as if it was a real person, similar to how Google Assistant or Siri works. However, instead of using voice, you typed.

The goal of this project was not only to manage intern schedules, but also to better understand how NLP worked so that we could use it in later applications. To get this to work, we had two undergrad interns and two part-time PhD interns.

It took about six months of work to get our bot up and running. While it served a needed purpose for our team (knowing when interns would be working vs in class), it was an extremely complex solution to a simple problem. We could have easily purchased a white board and had interns write their schedules there, making updates when things changed.

During this time, my team was also working on a project that used AI to detect what crops were growing where. This knowledge was extremely valuable to the company's supply chain and sales team. Knowing what crops are growing and where allows the company to position products where they would be needed most, while also helping the sales team know what customers to talk to.

During the project kick-off, it was estimated that this AI crop detection tool could increase sales in certain regions by up to ten million dollars.

These are just two examples of the ten total projects my team was working on. One other project had a large potential valuation of multiple millions in increased revenue, while all the others had nominal impact across the corporation. Most of them were tools to increase organization or shave a few hours of time off only a few people's jobs.

This is what I mean by spreading your work out across too many projects. Had I focused my team of interns on the two largest projects that had the highest return, we could have proven our value much, much quicker. However, we spent almost eight months working on too much work just to try and prove to others in the company we could be "innovative."

Companies are always looking for innovation. But innovation only matters when you build something that people will pay money for. You see this every year at CES. Companies develop new and innovative products, only to see lackluster sales and the eventual discontinuing of those products.

These two examples show various ways in which you can spread your impact too thin. It's best to focus on projects that will make a difference and go all in on them. Had my team focused on those two projects, we could have made a $25-30 million dollar increase in revenue for the company. That would have had a massive impact. Instead, we worked on projects that saved the company a few thousand dollars.

The goal of this section is to get your work week down to 20 hours a week. In these 20 hours, you will be providing more impact to your team / department / corporation than you currently are at 40 hours a week.

To most everyone reading this book, 20 hours is going to seem like a drastic cut from 40. But there is intentionality behind this. Let's take a look at some history and key stats to illustrate the benefit of working 20 hours a week.

The reason we're looking to get to 20 hours a week is simple: those who work 20 hours a week are twice as productive as those who work 35 (15). This is true because time constraints generate more creativity and innovation (16). Why? Because you're doing deliberate work. The time constraint forces you to cut out the work that doesn't matter and to focus on what does, which provides massive impact to the organization you work with.

The eight-hour workday was introduced by Henry Ford in the early 1900s. These hours were introduced as a way to attract autoworkers who were currently working 12-hour shifts. In the 1940s, the 40-hour work week became U.S. Law.

That's 81 years since we've passed a law stating that full time work = 40 hours a week. How many other things exist in your life that haven't changed over the past 80 years? Try and think of a few, I bet your list is pretty short.

A study done by AtTask titled "The State of Enterprise Work," (17) found that employees generally spend their 40 hours in three ways:

- 45% = Primary Job Duties.
- 40% = Meetings, Administrative Tasks, and "Interruptions."
- 14% = Email.

In getting down to 20 hours a week, we're looking to refine that 40% down to activities that provide value to your career. And then fiercely protecting the rest of your work time to not let invaluable and unnecessary activities creep back in.

So not only are you trying to cut out the fluff from your job, you're looking to constrain yourself to force creativity. Constraints provide focus and a creative challenge that will motivate you towards new, innovative ideas for products, services, or a business's process.

So how do we get there? How do we get to the 20 hours a week?

First up, we need to cut out all of the bullshit you're doing that's not providing value. Here are some examples...

- Town halls or large corporate-wide meetings.

- Any meeting in which you are not a decision-maker.
- Any meeting that is just for project updates.

Any project in which your actions can't be explicitly measured to show value.

Oftentimes, these things are not helping you progress towards your Why, but are instead busywork that's unnecessary and lacks purpose in your role.

Here is a visual of what you should aspire to. Your energy needs to be focused toward one large goal. This visual represents the half-ass on the left and a whole-ass effort on the right.

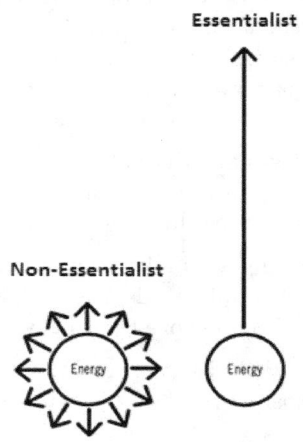

(Image source: Essentialism by Great McKeown)

How do we get to the one straight-arrow above? How do we focus our energy on one goal?

First up, select the project or piece of work that you determine has the most impact. Impact being cost savings or revenue gains. If you have multiple, pick something that you REALLY enjoy doing.

Now, we're going to cut out the rest of the noise.

You might be thinking, "Brandon, if I stop doing certain parts of my job, people will get mad." You are correct, they will, but their memories are short. Also, you're not going to "just stop doing them," you're going to find someone else to take over the work.

Depending on how much stuff you have on your plate, this process could take some time. The important thing is to begin the process. If you don't make attempts to cut out the noise, you won't move forward at all.

Let's go through a scenario of what this looks like. Let's imagine you're a Business Analyst and you've been assigned the three tasks below...

1. Analyze competitor's market share of new product X. This review will help determine if your company is to launch a competing product.

2. Set up a meeting with 20 people to share the results from a previous study.

3. Attending three result-sharing meetings of colleagues about different product lines. Each meeting is one-and-a-half hours each.

Of the three items above, the first bullet is the only one you should do. Why? Because it has a real impact on the company. From this analysis, your company will decide if it should launch a competing product OR if they should launch a product at all. Without this research, your company could end up wasting tens of thousands or millions of dollars. Put your focus solely on this research and crush it.

The other two items you should schedule away or look for someone to hand it off to. Here's how...

For bullet two, you should look to find an administrative assistant in your department who can help you with this. Even if the assistant doesn't report to you, they are often quite helpful and willing to support you in this type of task. It may seem small, but just setting up this meeting could waste several hours of your time.

In the third bullet, simply inform your colleagues that you aren't able to attend, but definitely want a copy of the presentation to read on your own time.

If you attend all three of the meetings, you'll easily waste an entire work day. But if you receive copies or notes of the presentations, you could consume all 3 of them in an hour and email questions to the presenter or, if need be, set a meeting time to discuss.

Just by eliminating these two tasks we've now saved one-and-a-half days of work. If you also cut out the town hall and other meetings where you weren't required to make decisions, you most likely have saved two to two-and-a-half days of work. That's 20 hours of work.

Even though you now have saved 20 hours, you should still shy away from working the full 40... The goal isn't to fill that time back up with other things. We need to protect that time, and help keep your mind sharp.

To help with this, block off the first 90 minutes to two hours of your day for heads-down work. Use this time when your brain is fresh and free of a day's worth of stress to accomplish meaningful tasks.

Meaningful tasks are NOT answering/sending emails. Meaningful tasks are doing the research mentioned in the bullet point above. During this time, turn off notifications and keep out of your email. Focus solely on completing the tasks that will bring your company the most value.

Emails are not meaningful because they typically do not require peak brain operation to do well. Most emails are simple exchanges of information, not complex research, evaluation, or creativity. If you are trying to portray something complex in an email, you should set up a meeting to discuss. Don't waste quality brain energy on something you can do later in the day.

Regardless of how well you optimize your schedule and tell people what you're doing, you're still going to get invited to a lot of meetings.

Remember, a good meeting is one where decisions are made. If you're constantly meeting to share progress updates, you're not using your time wisely. Caveat – sometimes you should call a meeting to celebrate a win or someone's birthday. Those are okay.

Next time you get invited to a meeting, ask yourself this question:

Am I required to make a decision during this meeting?

If you are unsure, reply to the person inviting you with this message–

Hello {Meeting Organizer},

I hope you're doing well today. Can you answer two quick questions about this meeting?

1 - What decision do we need to make in this meeting?

2 - Am I required to make any of these decisions?

Thanks for your help,

{Your Name}

With this email, you're going to get one of two answers. Yes, you're needed to make a decision. In which case, go to the meeting.

If you are told that you're not needed or no decisions are being made, here is a quick reply you can send:

Thanks for the quick reply!

I'd love to attend, but I've got some higher priority work that I'm assigned. Could you send me the deck and meeting notes once the meeting is done? I'll follow up if I have any questions.

That's it. It's that simple to start cutting out work and putting your activity towards things that matter. Remember, things that matter are the tasks that help you move towards successful completion of your mission. If a task isn't aligned with the mission, it shouldn't be made important.

For example, when I started writing this book, I had a lot of other items going on in my coaching business. I was making instructional videos for LinkedIn/Instagram daily, along with engaging/commenting on posts I found of interest on both platforms. On top of that, I was doing onboarding calls and reviewing applications. I stopped every single one of those items so that I could focus solely on writing this book. That was my mission. I know this book would provide immense value to those who purchased it and I wanted to make sure it was brought to its fullest potential. Those other activities were simply a distraction from me completing this book.

In the beginning, it may feel awkward to say no and cut work out. But don't fret. Your co-workers have a short memory, and once they start seeing your massive impact, they'll flock to you asking how they can do it, too.

As you grow in your career and start managing people, it will become even more important that your schedule is free. As a mid-level employee, I spent a lot of my time in meetings. I was there to provide data on projects that I or my team was working on, help make decisions, and keep people on their timelines.

As I moved into higher level positions, I immediately started to clear up my calendar. It was important that I was available to help my team when they needed me most, which often was spontaneously. Either to help put out a "fire" or sway a decision in an important meeting. My calendar started each day quite open, but over the course of the day, it would fill up.

However, it was still important that I continue to block my schedule for doing real work, and also for reflection. Each morning, I'd sit down and work on various components of my role for 60-90 minutes. I did this uninterrupted. Then each afternoon, I'd have 30-60 minutes blocked for reflection and thought about the happenings of that day/week/month. This time allowed me to connect the dots across multiple projects/people/tasks that I may have previously missed in the moment.

As you move up in your corporation, you're going to need to spend more time developing your team's skills, putting out fires, and managing various stakeholders. It's impossible for you to do that if you spend your entire day in meetings and let others control your schedule.

The only way this is possible at a higher level is to empower your team and those who report to you. As you move up, you're now being paid for your knowledge and ability to get things done. There is a difference in skill for sitting down and writing code as opposed to putting together a team of engineers. The company expects you to manage the output of the engineers, not write the code and make all the decisions for them. You need to elevate your thinking and output as you move up.

Putting This Into Action

- Cut out extra work immediately. Look at your calendar and see what you can scrap. Ex: Town halls.

- Find the one project you can focus on to provide massive impact and focus your time there.

- Stop working more than 40 hours a week. Ideally, get yourself to 20.

- Remember: People have short memories. Don't be afraid to tell them no.

Chapter 7: Agile to Improve Your Career

"Excellence is an art won by training and habituation. We do not act rightly because we have virtue or excellence, but we rather have those because we have acted rightly. We are what we repeatedly do. Excellence, then, is not an act but a habit." - Aristotle

Welcome to a crash course in the Agile Methodology. I'm going to cut out all the fluff that comes with how big corporations typically do Agile. Agile is meant to be simple. Agile is meant to help you build the right things, fast.

Most of you are probably familiar with using the Agile methodology at your corporation. It's a popular methodology for building software and running projects. In this chapter, we will lightly touch on that, but will spend most of our time on how to use the Agile methodology to plan out and enhance your career.

Here is the Agile mantra that I follow and teach:

- Think Big
- Start Small
- Scale Fast

Let's break this down…

Think Big: This is the large goal that you're hoping to get to. Let's say you have hopes of becoming a Director some day. That is your Think Big.

Start Small: Break down the Think Big into as many smaller tasks as you can think of. After each task, you should have something you can use/show someone for feedback.

Scale Fast: Rapidly build towards your Think Big in a small, but iterative way. Work on the tasks as quickly as you can and share them with someone, getting feedback each time you share it.

The opposite of Agile is called Waterfall. Sadly, waterfall is a methodology that is still followed by large corporations and many of its employees. Here is an illustration of what Waterfall looks like in practice:

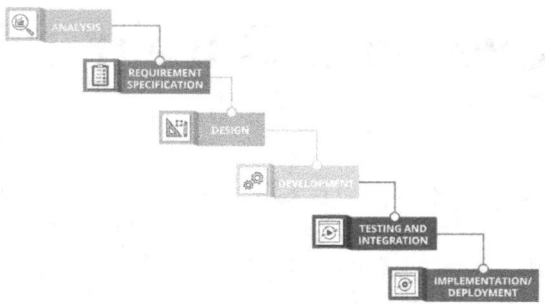

(Image source: The Cascading Costs of Waterfall by Jones + Waddell)

Each step of the Waterfall process is to be completed before moving on to the next step. This process typically creates tension between people working on each step. The people who are working in development expect that those in design and the steps before that have completed 100% of what they need to share with them.

Waterfall creates unrealistic expectations that are only met with failure. Why? Because it's impossible. You can't expect to go from one phase of the product to the next without there being re-work. Secondly, even if you do and you launch the product you were building, no customer has seen it nor have they given you feedback on if they'd actually use it.

One great example to understand the difference between Agile and Waterfall is with the "layered cake example." You have the opportunity to eat a layered cake in 2 ways: All the icing, then each layer at a time (Waterfall), or you can cut a slice of the whole thing, eating each slice until the whole cake is gone (Agile).

The reason the Waterfall methodology is so popular is due to its lack of rapid change and testing.

If there are two things that most corporate people hate the most: change and being proven wrong. Far too many people enjoy doing things "how they've always done it," because it's easier to do what they've always done than implement change. Changing something will require new ways of working/thinking/acting at work.

Agile changes all of this by introducing rapid change and empiricism. By definition Empiricism is:

> The theory that all knowledge is derived from sense-experience. Stimulated by the rise of experimental science, it developed in the 17th and 18th centuries, expounded in particular by John Locke, George Berkeley, and David Hume.

To simplify this, it means you make decisions based on data from observation. This causes issues in the corporate world because far too many times people push their "amazing idea" down through the workforce using persuasion or perceived power of seniority in a role.

Those types of people don't like being told when they're wrong or that an idea just isn't going to work. However, you're no better than they are if you just state, "This idea is dumb and won't work." But if you take an empirical approach and test the idea, bringing back data to prove why it won't work (or that there is a better idea), this shows you are using empirical data in your Agile process.

Empiricism comes into Agile when you start testing ideas. I'll share scenarios later in this chapter, but a great example of testing an idea is Kickstarter (crowdfunding website. www.kickstarter.com). Anyone can post a concept to Kickstarter and try to raise money to build their concept. If an idea gets money, then it proves people are interested in that idea. If it doesn't, then no one is interested. That is empirical evidence.

However, empirical data can get tricky. If you survey 10 people and ask them which brand of cola they would buy, you've just learned how 10 people would respond to a survey about which cola they would buy. If you want to actually know what cola they will buy, you instead need to offer them a cola, and see which they buy.

This process of developing and analyzing empirical evidence is frustrating because a vast majority of the ideas we have just don't work for one reason or another. You don't gain confidence in the idea until you test it. This is where rapid change comes into play. Once you start testing out a bunch of ideas, things change quickly because you get vast amounts of data that inspires more testing, taking you down paths you may not have been down before.

It's much, MUCH simpler to just come up with an idea and then work towards building that idea than it is to test 100s of items to make sure you build the RIGHT THING.

When someone comes up with a new idea, it tends to get attached to their ego. After you spend time working in a particular industry for long enough, you feel that you've become an expert. So once you come up with a new idea, it's easy to attach that idea to your emotions or ego. Once you're an expert, you can't be wrong... right?

The problem is, far too many people act in this capacity. Especially those who are well-educated. Once you receive your Bachelors, Master's, or PhD, you tend to stop looking for evidence that proves something you've done is incorrect. This lack of evidence-seeking is connected to ego. Most don't want to damage their ego by being proven wrong.

This way of thinking is so prevalent that science has given it a term: Cognitive Dissonance. This term is used to describe the mental discomfort that results from holding two conflicting beliefs, values, or attitudes (18). As mentioned above, people struggle with change, so much so that inconsistency in beliefs will cause people to engage in actions that will minimize this feeling of discomfort.

This discomfort drives people to then reject, explain away, or simply avoid new information. An example of this that took place on the world stage was the 2020 election, where former United States President Donald Trump consistently lied about having lost the election, despite evidence to the contrary.

Not only is this found in the highest elected office in the United States, but also in the courtrooms. Here is an excerpt from an article (19) in The New York Times discussing the murder of a 16-year old female:

> "In Nassau County on Long Island, after DNA evidence showed that the sperm in a 16-year-old murder victim did not come from the man convicted of the crime, prosecutors argued that it must have come from a consensual lover, even though her mother and best friend insisted she was a virgin. In Florida, after DNA showed that the pubic hairs at the scene of a rape did not belong to the convicted rapist, prosecutors argued that the hairs found on the victim's bed could have come from movers who brought furniture to the bedroom a week or so earlier."

This example is extreme, but is a clear case of cognitive dissonance. The evidence does not connect to the beliefs of the prosecutors, so they are trying to clearly explain away or ignore it. In the United States, it's estimated that six percent of the prison population is wrongly convicted.

If it's possible that in extreme cases where evidence is clear and concise for someone to still be in disbelief, it's easy to see how this too can happen in the corporate world where often stakes are much, much smaller.

In the corporate world, if an idea ends up being bad or someone makes a mistake, it's a negative towards that person's ego. So rather than give up on the idea or admit they were wrong, they'll blame others, push more marketing dollars, or convince someone they need more money because they need another feature to make the idea whole.

This process wastes millions, if not billions, of dollars each year in the corporate world.

This same process is what holds back your career. You need to be willing to experiment and test out ideas as often as you can. Not only will it help you advance your career faster, you'll learn faster because of it.

How To Design An Experiment

While using Agile Methodology, you want evidence to help show what you're building will solve a problem. Getting someone to simply say "Yes, I like this" isn't enough evidence.

To get evidence, you'll want to design an experiment. An experiment starts with a hypothesis. Hypotheses follow a simple format:

**If I/We {do something} for {user} they
will {respond a certain way}.**

Here is an example: If we send a pre-read 2 days before a meeting for executives, they will read it and not require a 15-minute project debrief every meeting.

Now that you have your hypothesis, you need to test it. To do this, you need an experimental group and a control group. The experimental group will be getting the pre-read, while the control group has nothing change (ie: gets no pre-read).

To test this, you can send a pre-read to the experimental group 2 days in advance and then attend the meeting and record which executives asked for a project debrief to start the meeting.

In doing this, you'll learn if the pre-read helps avoid a project debrief. Or you could find that the executives didn't read the pre-read anyhow. In which case you can redo your hypothesis and try the experiment again. This time sending in 3 days in advance, as possibly, 2 days wasn't enough time.

It's important to not let either group know they are involved in an experiment. Doing so will invalidate your results because it could let bias creep into your test.

When you embrace difficulties, you learn and retain information better. That is what Agile Methodology is going to do for you. It's going to put you on a path to learning faster and building skills that will help you attain the career you're after.

Now that you understand more of the why, let's jump into the specifics of how to actually practice in an Agile manner.

When people talk about Agile, they often talk about building software/apps/digital stuff. It's widely used for that (often incorrectly (20)) and those are not the only ways in which you can use Agile. Let's rehash the mantra–

- Think Big
- Start Small
- Scale Fast

There are a few technical components of Agile Methodology that are important to know. Here are six basic terms to learn.

**Note: Most often Agile is done as a team. So part of these definitions below speak to that.

Backlog: List of all the items of work that need to get done for a given product.

Sprint Planning: A meeting time where you sit down and plan everything you're going to do for the upcoming sprint.

Sprint: The amount of time it takes to create one product increment. A product increment would be a "Start Small" item. This is usually done in one to two week increments. The product would be your "Think Big."

Stand Up: A daily meeting where a team talks about what they did yesterday, what they're going to do today, and anything that is blocking them from getting work done.

Sprint Review: A meeting where you sit down and review everything that was completed during the Sprint.

Retrospective: A meeting at the end of a Sprint where the team talks about what went well, what didn't, and where they can improve.

Now that we understand some basic terminology, I'll string them together so you can see the cadence.

When you start off on your Think Big, you'll want to break down the different items or to-do tasks. As you write out these items, you'll want to put them in some sort of order.

Ex: Do A first, then B, then C. This sorted list is your Backlog. Your Backlog is never firm. It's always fluid. As you learn, you can put new items, remove items or reorganize items on your Backlog.

Once you have a list of items, you'll then pick the first one and plan out everything you need to do to accomplish that item. Doing this is your Sprint Planning.

Once you have the items planned, it's time to get to work. You'll want to set a deadline for how long you have to do this work. Your deadline should be one to two weeks in length. This will be your Sprint. You want to set a short-term deadline so that you force yourself to get started on the work sooner than later. If you set a deadline of a month, you'll procrastinate and the quality of work will suffer.

As you start each day, it's good to review what you accomplished the day before and what you plan to do that day. Reviewing your work keeps your progress fresh and helps set the stage for your next pieces of work. I like to accomplish my toughest tasks first when my brain is fresh. If I have a blocker, I work on that until it's no longer stopping me from moving forward. Consider this your Stand Up.

Once you're done with the work and the task(s) of the Sprint are complete, you should do a self-reflective Sprint Review and Retrospective together. Look at all that you've accomplished and celebrate it. Take yourself out to lunch or grab a drink after work. Celebrate that you moved forward on your career or project.

It's important to celebrate your successes and accomplishments. Doing this helps keep your energy high and shows you that you're accomplishing something each week, or every other week. Remember, when you're positive/happy, your output is increased by 31%(21). That's not a small number to ignore.

With Waterfall, celebration doesn't really happen until the end. You may spend a year or two building a project and then seeing it be released for users to actually use. You could celebrate your work along the way, however, you didn't actually finish anything. The entire product with Waterfall isn't complete until the last step. With Agile, you have something complete at the end of each Sprint.

As you review, take some Time to be self-reflective on things that went well, things you should stop doing, or how you could improve your work for the next week. Ex: You attended too many meetings that didn't align with your Sprint objectives, so in the next Sprint, you'll work on attending less meetings.

If the plan for implementing agile is unclear, go back and re-read the section on terminology. It's important to understand each step.

Let's look at an in-depth example of how you could use Agile to help improve a process in your department. Remember: Think Big, Start Small, Scale Fast.

What is a Product?

A product is any item or service you sell to serve a customer's need or want. Note: selling doesn't always refer to money exchange. It could be exchange of time, data, or money.

Anything that you create could be deemed a product. A couple of examples–

- The weekly analytics email you send to your department each Friday
- Your companies recruiting process
- Your career
- The app your team is building
- The Design System from the Product Team
- How you teach leadership skills to others in your organization
- The monthly update call you run for senior leadership

To elaborate further, the weekly analytics email serves a customer's need, where the customer is the department you sent it to. In exchange, they are giving you their time to read it and use the data. However, if no one was doing either of those two things, the product wouldn't have value.

If you take that perspective, it gives you the opportunity to develop and improve anything like a product.

Product Feature

A product feature is part of a product. For example, Instagram is a product, posting a video would be a feature. Posting a picture, making a comment, hearting, sharing...all features.

Scenario 1: Jill works in the recruiting department at her corporation. Jill thinks she can improve the satisfaction of both the candidates and the hiring managers by improving the communication process. To make sure she develops the best possible solution, she's going to use the Agile Methodology.

In the recruiting process (product), there are currently multiple components (features). There is the job description, the website that hosts the job description, the initial screening call, the in-person/video interview with the hiring manager, the follow up interviews, the background check, and finally, the offer.

Think Big: Jill wants to restructure the ENTIRE recruiting process and fix the negative feedback the recruiting team has received for each of the recruiting process components above.

Start Small: Jill is going to start small by picking just one component of the recruiting process to fix.

Not knowing which component would be most valuable to fix first, Jill decides to poll the hiring managers and her recruiting peers, asking them which of the steps in the hiring process is most stressful to them. When analyzing feedback, it's clear that communication with candidates is the number one issue.

To get started, Jill calls an hour-long meeting with her recruiting peers to brainstorm ideas for the issues they currently have with communication, for example, scheduling interviews.

During the brainstorming session, Jill learns from other recruiters that text messaging is becoming a preferred way for both hiring managers and candidates to interact.

To see if text messaging would work in her organization, Jill decides to design an experiment to test her idea.

To get started on her experiment, Jill creates her hypothesis — If we (hiring managers) schedule interviews over text messages with our candidates, they will respond quicker and interviews will be scheduled faster.

Jill kicks off the experiment by choosing one job posting to test against. She splits candidates into two groups and decides to hold the experiment for one week. One of them communicates with the hiring manager to schedule an interview over text message, the other continues using email.

To help validate if this process works well, Jill will monitor how quickly interviews are set up after a text message or email is sent. She also plans to send a survey to the hiring manager and candidate after one week to determine which process each group liked better.

After monitoring the results and sending the surveys, Jill discovered using text messages results in interviews being scheduled 42% faster. In the survey, hiring managers noted that text messages are easier to manage than trying to sort through emails in their inbox.

Now that Jill has seen success in this solution, she may decide to test it with a larger audience to see if she can replicate the results. Regardless, she has a repeatable process to help validate new ideas using the Agile Methodology.

This repeatable process = Define a problem, develop a hypothesis, run an experiment.

Scale Fast: Now Jill needs to continue improving the recruiting process. This repeatable process is how Jill can now scale fast. She will need to continue running experiments rapidly to test out and implement new solutions. Once she has confidence that something works well, she will build a team to help implement the idea.

In this scenario, she may need to connect with someone from the IT department to implement a text messaging platform that all hiring managers can use.

By using data and testing, you increase the opportunity to build something that actually works and creates impact in your organization. This is exactly what Jill did. This experiment example could have easily turned out the opposite. That candidates were quicker to schedule by email and hiring managers preferred email as well.

However, Jill had no way to know which solution was better until she tested it. Had she just implemented a new solution and caused a mass shift in communication and scheduling, she may have created more issues and made everyone in the entire process even unhappier.

Let's go through another example of using Agile. This one is around culture change. It's short, but it's punchy in effectively illustrating how you can use Agile to help improve your organization.

Rob is the CEO at a mid-sized manufacturing firm. He wants to help his company become more innovative by getting employees to use the Agile Methodology. The Agile Methodology will allow the teams in Rob's company to test out their ideas quicker, helping to find the ones their customers will like faster than before.

Think Big: Rob wants to make the company more innovative and is going to implement the Agile Methodology in his corporation. Whether Rob is a mid-level employee or a CEO, he would take the same approach as Jill did above.

Start Small: He begins by testing this out on ONE TEAM. He works with this group to try and shift their work and their practices towards the Agile Methodology.

Rob first offers a full Agile Methodology training, emphasizing flexibility in implementing these new, different steps. He tells his team, "Okay, now that we have an understanding of Agile Methodology, we're going to try it out. But I don't expect you to do it all at once. We're going to start by doing just standups. Let's plan to meet at my desk each day this week at nine in the morning. At the end of the week, we can do a quick discussion on how you felt it went."

Scale Fast: Once the team is comfortable with standups, they may then graduate into a retrospective or starting to break work into two-week sprints. Over time, the team works up to doing the full Agile Methodology.

As Rob's team starts to feel confident in how the Agile Methodology is working, Rob starts to share this method with other teams.

Scaling fast doesn't mean Rob immediately switches his whole company to Agile Methodology. From the initial team, he only learned how it would affect that team. A gradual next step would be to scale to another team, then maybe a department.

Rob continues to iterate through this rollout until he has widespread adoption. Maybe you go from one team to two, then two to three, or two to eight and then eight to an entire department. Eventually, you get change (complete rollout) throughout the entire corporation.

But, the great part of going this route is that you uncover new findings with each new team. Every time you try and scale, you learn of new roadblocks and have new things to share. If you were to try and do ALL of this at once, you ultimately fail, as you'd run into huge roadblocks immediately, some large enough that you can't get over.

Notice how both of these examples didn't include any digital or tech based development. Agile is more than just a fancy way to build software and apps.

I've given you two scenarios in how you can use Agile to improve a process or implement a new one. Right now you might be asking yourself: *How is Agile going to help me personally in my career?*

In the last chapter, we learned about creating massive impact. To do this, you need to work in an Agile way. Otherwise, you're just guessing at what may or may not work. By working this way, you'll wind up spending a lot of time on massive projects with very little return. There is the slim chance you get lucky and hit a home run on a massive project, but it's unlikely. Your odds are much greater using the Agile methodology, as Agile projects have an average of double the success rate of Waterfall. Agile provides plenty of opportunities for you to create massive impact for your organization, thus giving you the notoriety necessary to help with promotions.

However, you shouldn't only use Agile on projects. You should view your career through the Agile lens as well, where your Think Big is a promotion to becoming a Director, your Start Small is buying this book, and your Scaling Fast is quickly implementing the learnings of this book.

Throughout implementing the learnings of this book, you need to be testing along the way. For example, once you develop your Why statement, you begin with trying out different versions with co-workers to see which one creates the greatest emotional response. It's important to keep in mind that your Why may change over time (this is ok and natural) which will require retesting the new versions.

To keep your career moving forward, make it a habit to constantly test out new concepts, noting how you can continually increase your impact and value to the organization. If you stop testing, and therefore stop learning, you become stagnant and allow others to pass you. It's similar to large organizations who continue the Waterfall process and find themselves way behind smaller companies with more Agile startups.

Agile gives you the opportunity to build and share your work with someone every Sprint. Not only are you incrementally building towards your Think Big, but you're given the opportunity to celebrate wins. You're able to celebrate because you're completing something each week. These small celebrations go a long way in keeping up your emotional well being and keeping you excited to accomplish your goals.

I'll end this chapter with a few of my favorite quotes that help hammer home the point of being Agile–

"I have not failed. I've just found 10,000 ways that won't work."

- Thomas Edison

"Success is the ability to go from failure to failure without losing your enthusiasm."

- Winston Churchill

"Only those who dare to fail greatly can ever achieve greatly."

- Robert F. Kennedy

"If you're not prepared to be wrong, you'll never come up with anything original."
- Ken Robinson

Putting This Into Action

- Think Big: Find one goal that you can set as your Think Big. This could be a work project or the next step in your career.

- Start Small: Make a list of tasks you'll need to complete to accomplish your think big. Try to list them all out, high level is okay. Pick the top item(s) from the list that you can do now and can complete in 1-2 weeks.

  - At the end of the 1-2 weeks, you need to have a tangible result. Something to show you made progress.

  - Planning is not progress. Do something. Research, sketching, or build a small prototype.

- Scale Fast: As with the example of Jill and Rob, they created a process that was scalable. Use that process to scale quickly.

- Structure your week in an Agile way. Reread the definitions of Agile Terms if necessary.

Chapter 8: Ask For Forgiveness, Not Permission

"It's better to get forgiveness than permission." - Grace Hopper

Getting permission to do something is one of the biggest hurdles you can face in your career. It used to be a constant hurdle for me, until I stopped asking… I realized that every time I asked for permission it would amplify my timeline of getting anything done.

Permission vs. forgiveness is all about how to take calculated risks. It's not simply bypassing your boss and starting to make a bunch of unilateral decisions. Rather, it's learning to make calculated decisions to help you have massive impact in your role.

For a majority of you reading this book, your boss would prefer that you operate autonomously without constantly coming to them for requests.

Some of you might be saying, "No way man… Not my boss. They constantly force me to ask them for permission." If that's the case, then you have a micromanaging boss. Go back to chapter six and review the part on dealing with a micromanaging boss. They are forcing you to ask permission because they don't trust you. Take ownership and fix it.

This topic brings up a certain degree of hesitancy. If you're used to asking for permission, going and doing can seem a bit scary. Especially because getting in trouble at work is stressful. Your job is your livelihood. It's how you put food on the table. That's why I noted that this is about taking calculated risks, not just doing whatever you want.

Once you learn to start taking these calculated risks and asking for forgiveness rather than permission, you'll start getting tasks done way faster, completing projects with more impact than you thought possible.

As mentioned before, one of my previous roles was to open an Innovation Lab for a large agricultural company. I want to show you how I spent $15 that wound up saving the company over $100,000.

This lab was meant to build prototypes or MVPs (minimum viable products), to help prove out a new idea quickly and cheaply. It wasn't meant to build production level applications or to build fancy tools the whole company used. Nor was it meant to be bug-free. It was meant to purely test out a concept and prove if it was worth investing additional time or money.

To cut down on cost and to test rapidly, we hired a bunch of interns instead of full-timers. All of the work we did was digital.

My team would often work with other departments. In this scenario we were tasked with building a new web app that would do calculations on data that was uploaded from a spreadsheet. The calculations would then display the data back to the user in a visual way so they could make decisions. It was a very simple web app, nothing fancy. In fact, it only took about three days to develop.

To let others test out the web app, we needed a server, and to get a server, we had to fill out a form. The form was a headache, with confusing, technical writing aimed at an audience completely unlike me or my interns. It was written for someone who had advanced knowledge of security protocols.

After filling out the form, we'd have to schedule a meeting with 3 different people to review the form and make sure data wasn't missing.

Sadly, I didn't know how long the process to get a server would take until I was sitting in that initial meeting. I submitted the form on a Monday, and was able to schedule a review meeting for that Friday. That's four days of doing nothing... In that meeting, I learned two things:

1.   I missed some information on the form and would have to fill it out again and resubmit it.

2.   Even after I get the form right, it'll take another five to six weeks before I get my server.

Spending 4 days waiting for the meeting felt like eternity to me. Having to wait another 5-6 weeks to actually get the server sounded awful. It sounded like a lot of wasted time where my project wouldn't move forward and my team couldn't create meaningful impact for the organization.

I'm sure you can relate with a process similar to this in your company. A process that is overly bureaucratic and doesn't really provide much benefit to the organization.

Once I realized this entire process would take five to eight weeks to get my server, I decided to take control of the situation: I purchased my own server. I went to the Amazon AWS website, found a low-tier server that would run us about $15 a month, and ordered it.

Making that purchase was a calculated risk. Here are the factors I took into account in making this decision:

- A $15 expense to a billion dollar revenue company was the equivalent to 1/1,000th of a penny.

- The data that our app was displaying wasn't protected or confidential. If it leaked, no one was getting fired and the company wasn't losing any intellectual property.

- My team built a simple login that protected random people from accessing the data.

- The cost (my salary calculated at an hourly rate) it took for myself to fill out that initial form, plus attending those meetings, was significantly greater than $15.

- The cost it took for others to review the form, attend meetings, and create our server for us was significantly greater than $15.

Looking at those bullets, you can see how this decision was low-risk. However, most employees are scared to make a purchase on behalf of the company fearing retribution from their manager or employer.

In this scenario, I didn't just make any purchase. I made one that was going to move the company forward. Not only did it help complete a project in under a week, it saved the company thousands on resources.

Had my boss or another superior asked me to justify my actions, I could have broken down the cost savings based on estimated salaries of those on the project, while also showing them how quickly we were able to complete the project.

The work we did on this project also had compounding effects. Once the requesting team had a chance to use the prototype, they realized the effort to prepare data to be uploaded to our tool was much more work than originally anticipated.

While the tool worked as expected, we proved that continued development on the tool wouldn't provide the company any financial benefit. The team then decided to continue using their current tool, and we stopped development on the one we built.

Prior to my team working on this prototype, the requesters had talked with a vendor about building a tool that would be an add-on to their current tool. That add-on was going to do exactly what our prototype did. We built it and proved it's low value in less than a week. The consultants estimated building an add-on was going to cost around $100,000. Had we not proven the value of this request was low in a timely manner, the team would have proceeded in spending $100,000 to build out the tool add-on.

Again, in spending $15, we saved the company over $100,000. The ROI (Return On Investment) on that little project was ~633,000%.

Let's look at another scenario of calculated risk, one where I decided to follow company process and not move forward without the proper authorization.

During that same period at the Innovation Lab, I was consulting for a different team from another department in our organization. This team was looking to do a complete refresh of its software user interface. To do this successfully, we needed to work with an outside vendor as our current teams didn't have the expertise to handle the work.

After meeting with multiple vendors and vetting them on their skills and price, the team and I found a vendor we liked. The total project cost would be ~$1,000,000. The work they had done for other companies was impeccable. They were highly skilled and one of the top in their field. We were really excited to get started with them on the project.

However, signing this contract without approval was not a risk I was going to take. It needed to be prepared and submitted to our procurement team for review and proper signatures.

Could I have signed it and engaged with the company to start the work? Absolutely. Was it a calculated risk I was willing to take? No.

Here is why:

- It's a ~$1,000,000 contract.
- The company requires authorization for any spending over $10,000.
- It's a ~$1,000,000 contract.

The risk to reward on this calculation was not a risk I was willing to take. Had I previously signed contracts for $20,000 or even $90,000 without procurement approval? Yes, because, I had high confidence in the ROI of the project.

When you look to ask for forgiveness and not permission, it's all about evaluating your position in the company. For some, a $15 expense may sound risky. For others, signing a million dollar contract is a monthly, or even weekly occurrence.

For your role, you need to find a balance. Will you do something that will get your hand slapped once you ask for forgiveness? Yes. Are there other times you will be rewarded for moving forward and not taking the time to ask permission? Yes.

If you end up getting a strange email/text/instant message from your boss and you are quite certain you're going to get your hand slapped for something that you did, set up a time to meet them in person (or video), and be the first person to start the conversation. Immediately say something like, "Forgive me, for I have sinned," or, "Bless me, I have sinned." This is a little tip I picked up from FBI Hostage Negotiator Chris Voss (22).

By starting the conversation with a joke, it lightens the mood. It shows an awareness of the situation by immediately acknowledging instead of defending or attacking. It's seeing $15 as actually $15, instead of making it feel like it's $1,000,000.

Here's a quick checklist to keep in mind as you engage in risk evaluation. These questions offer a baseline to help guide your discernment towards risk-taking:

- What have you done before that you didn't ask permission and your hand didn't get slapped? Can you assign a monetary value to it?

- What have you seen your peers do before that didn't get them in trouble?

- Think back to a time when you DID get your hand slapped. What was the cause?

- What actions have you seen others take that got them in trouble?

Getting more intentional with risk-taking will set you apart in your company, as far too many people are scared to take even the smallest risks. Fifteen-dollar risks. It's the same reason that Agile is bastardized across so many large corporations.

Asking for forgiveness and Agile are closely related. Each time you ask for forgiveness, you take a risk. Each time you come up with a new idea and run an experiment, you take a risk. However, if you are never willing to take risk, to test failure, then you'll never move ahead. You'll never learn what works or what doesn't.

Putting This Into Action

- Start taking calculated risks.

- Increase your risk taking until you get your hand slapped. This helps you understand your boundaries.

- Use your judgement. I.e.: Don't sign a $1M contract if you don't typically have authority...

Section 2 Checkpoint

Hopefully, you're starting to see the building blocks of this method coming together. First, we covered mindset to help make sure you were mentally in the right place. This included things like taking ownership, getting over your ego, and truly connecting with others by using empathy and having a strong Why. This shift in mindset created the foundation for you to gain followers.

By working smarter, you'll start to streamline your days and increase the amount of financial benefit you bring back to the company. That's what massive impact truly is — how much money can you generate or save the company.

But that is not something you can do alone. You need to work with your followers to deliver this impact together with you at the lead. With that, let's reflect on changes you're starting to see in your role/career—

- You've found a lot more time in your day to complete true work.
- You're focusing on massive impact. You've stopped working on multiple projects and are focusing your energy to bring better value.
- You are able to articulate a Think Big that you're working on.
- Data has become your new go-to buzzword for presenting and refuting ideas.
- You have or are working towards getting your hand slapped.
- Most importantly, you've gained followers. You know who they are because they're there when you need them, support your new missions, and help you on projects in ways others haven't before.

If some of that reflection doesn't resonate, it means you're not implementing your new knowledge (or it's your first time through the book). Do something, try something, learn from it.

The number one mistake you can make with continued education is to not implement or test out the new stuff you learn. It's something I see far too often in people trying to get ahead. They read, they attend seminars, they get certifications, they get an advanced degree. They then sit on that accomplishment and don't put their new knowledge to the test.

Every item you learn in this book, you should try out for yourself. The scenarios in this book are meant to give you real world examples that will help you understand how to test your ideas. Even if you think you might not be 100% correct in your understanding, try it anyhow. Getting started is infinitely better than being right.

Finding ways to have massive impact in your career can be challenging. Especially when you're trying to implement new methodologies such as the Agile Methodology. My coaching program offers support in your endeavors and opportunity for group and 1x1 coaching to help get you through any roadblocks you may encounter when trying to deliver massive impact. If you're interested in gaining personalized support, you can fill out an application at www.dynamiccorporateleader.com/program-application.

Section 3: Building Teams

If you've implemented the first two sections successfully, you've most likely gained some followers by now. The response to your new mindset should be almost immediate. When you start taking ownership, people will notice. Especially if you haven't acted in this manner before.

Depending on where you are in your career and how much of a mindset shift you've had to make, you should begin to notice change within two to four weeks. It won't take long for people to recognize that you are caring for them and supporting their work in new ways.

The only caveat to this is any potential damage you've done previously. If you've been an arrogant asshole to your co-workers, the newfound you will take some time to grow on them. That's ok. Make sure to own it. Take ownership and acknowledge that you were a butthead before, but you're working hard to change.

If you are struggling to gain followers, go back and re-read the chapters on ownership and ego. If you're lacking followers, it's most likely because you're failing at these two. Your mindset and ability to work smarter are crucial attributes to you building strong teams.

I say this, because if you aren't strong in the mindset, you're going to struggle building teams. The same goes for working smarter. You'll be able to build teams, but your teams won't bring massive impact back to the organization.

To maximize the impact you can provide in your career and be able to move up the corporate ladder, you need to be able to build teams. Just having followers is not enough, although they certainly play a role in team building. Your followers are going to be there to support you and will join your team when called upon, but to obtain the skills you need, you'll have to seek help outside your followers.

The great thing is, with the skills from Section one and two, you're in a great position to recruit people to your teams, whether this is a new hire outside the organization or someone from within that you'll pull into a project.

Being able to build teams to help support your mission or project is imperative to your success. Being able to build a team will amplify the impact you can have across the organization. Do you remember the proverb we opened the first section with?

If you want to go fast, go alone

If you want to go far, go together

Now that we understand how to build followers and work smart, we need to amplify our impact by building a team. In the last section of this book, we're going to go in-depth and discuss how to get the most out of others and how to have a 1x1.

If you want to stay true to the proverb, you need to be able to get the most of those around you and those you place on your teams. As noted before, the higher you move in an organization, the less "daily activities" you have, and the more skilled you need to be at unifying the talent of others.

By the time you're ready to implement what you'll learn in this section, you'll have many followers. This section is going to show you how to unite your followers and to utilize (or develop) their skills to do good for the organization. Ultimately, you're creating an environment that allows for freedom of expression and innovation, where people feel safe exploring and attempting the impossible.

Chapter 9: Getting The Most Out Of Others

"Great things in business are never done by one person, they're done by a team of people." - Steve Jobs

In the first section of this book, you learned how to gain followers and truly connect with people. Now we're going to focus on using those followers and others in your organization to build teams and amplify the impact you can provide to your corporation.

This skill is a necessity for wanting to move up the career ladder. The further you go in your career, the more important skills for building and maximizing teams becomes.

For example, when you start your job as a Jr. Business Analyst/Programmer/ Designer/etc., you spend a large majority of your day analyzing/coding/ designing/etc.ing. That is what you were hired to do.

Now, think back to interactions you've had with your boss or a Director in your department. Do they spend their day analysing/programming/design- ing/etc.*ing*? No. Maybe a little, but a majority of their focus is towards people management and strategy. People management encompasses managing those who report to you, but also stakeholder management across the organization.

I'll revert to the wisdom of Liz Wiseman and Greg McKeown in teaching this concept through their book *Multipliers*. This book breaks down some technical ways to build teams and multiply the output of those on the team.

For the purpose of your work, a team can be a multitude of things. If you're a manager, it could be the people that report to you. Or you could be part of a team that your manager is leading. Or your team could be one that you put together.

Remember, job titles don't make you a leader. If you have a strong mission that excites others and they view you as a leader, you'll be able to build a team around you to help accomplish that mission.

Sadly many corporations are held back by bad managers. Many of you reading this book have most likely witnessed this firsthand. Unfortunately, the research backs this up. Here is a snippet from a study that was run in 2012 (23):

- Only 36% of Americans are happy at their job.

- 65% say a better boss would make them happier than a pay raise.

- 31% of employees feel uninspired and unappreciated by their boss. Close to 15% feel downright miserable.

- Close to 60% of Americans say they would do a better job if they got along better with their boss.

- Only 38% describe their boss as "great," with 42% saying their bosses don't work very hard, and close to 20% saying their boss has little or no integrity.

So what does this tell you? It doesn't tell you that people in the workforce hate their job and their bosses. It says they are desperately seeking inspiration and a leader they can get behind.

You can be that leader. That is what this book is trying to teach you. There is AMPLE opportunity to disrupt the workforce for the better. There are so many people looking for human connection at work and a leader they can admire and appreciate. Using the **Dynamic Corporate Leader Method**, you can become that leader.

You should be proud of what you do each day

I'm very proud of what I've done in my career. What I've done and how I've helped people isn't magic. It's something that can be learned and executed. I wouldn't have spent months writing this book if I didn't feel it could help someone advance their career from teachings in this book.

I shared a reference quote in a previous chapter. I want to share another because it aligns directly with what we're learning in this chapter:

> "Brandon is unlike any manager I have had before. From my very first interview, I could tell that Brandon's first priority was his

> people. His leadership style relies on trusting those under him to do what they do best while he unsures they have all the motivation and resources necessary to be successful. A combination of challenging his employees to be better, an eagerness to fight for them, and a willingness to admit when he's wrong makes Brandon an irreplaceable part of any team."

When you start to doubt what's possible, take a moment to reflect on successes you've already had in your career. Each of those successes came with frustration of learning and trying something new. This book and its lessons are no different. You got this.

According to Multipliers, there are two types of leaders: Multipliers & Diminishers.

I argue that in place of leaders, we should use the word Managers. Simply because the ways the authors speak of Leaders in this book is describing someone in a leadership position. Not someone who has followers. But what we're going to learn in this section falls under a blend of management and leadership.

So what is a Multiplier or Diminisher? Here are their traits:

- Multiplier excels at bringing teams together + maximizing talent, while a diminisher creates low output from others.
- Multipliers create an intense, yet inspiring place, while diminishers stifle and create tension.
- Multipliers challenge and push, while diminishers bark orders.
- Multipliers make room for debate and inspire debate, while diminishers always have the last word.
- Multipliers empower and invest in people, while diminishers micromanage.

To help quantify employees output the author's surveyed employees asking about their perceived output when working for a Multiplier or Diminisher. When working for a Diminisher, the Diminisher often received only 20-50% of their capability.

However, when working for a Multiplier, there is a 2x Multiplier Effect that comes into play. Employees reported that working for a Multiplier increased their capability to 70-100%.

Imagine what you can accomplish if you're getting 2x the output from those around you...

Just seeing the traits, you can clearly see the difference between these two types of people. As you think back to your career, I'm sure you can come up with at least a few names that could fall under either of those two sets.

From the names above, pull out a name of someone you thought was a Multiplier. I bet you worked with more passion, brought more energy, and were more creative in your problem solving. Not only did they get 100% from you, they also pushed for more. So not only do Multipliers get 70-100% their capability, they are good at pushing people to expand their current knowledge and grow, thus increasing the output they can get from one individual past 100%.

The interesting bit about these traits is that one person can float back and forth between both. It's possible to be part Multiplier and part Diminisher. This happens when you let things like Ego and Ownership slip. It's important to learn how to recognize these tendencies in ourselves so that we can learn how to do right and what to avoid.

Note** Keep in mind as you continue reading that everything shared in this book is something you can learn. Don't believe in the hype of "great leaders are born." Some people do have innate abilities to do the below. If that's not you, don't worry, you can learn this. Ex: I'm an introvert by nature. But by practicing the below, I got over my insecurities of being around people and excelled in ways most have not.

With each of the bullets above comes a step-by step-guide on how to best work as a multiplier. Let's jump into the first one.

Multipliers Excel At Bringing Teams Together + Maximizing Talent.

If you're looking to tackle a new project, building a quality team will help increase the impact that your project can have. The great part about this is that there is a method for building a great team.

When working to put together a team, look at the end goal of the project you want to create, then work backwards. Starting at the end helps you realize the steps you need to take to accomplish the project, and also the people required to make it happen.

Let's say you've been tasked with building a new mobile app. As you work backwards from the end goal of the app, you realize you'll need engineer(s), graphic designer(s), ux/ui designer(s), possibly a business analyst, and a copywriter.

Now that you know what you need, it's time to build your team. Here are the steps for building a high quality team:

Step 1: Look everywhere for talent. Throw away any traditional boundaries or hierarchies. If someone has a skill you like, go after them. Make sure to find diversity in your talent. Don't bring in all the same type of person/role/skills.

Step 2: Find the natural talent of a person. What is something they can do with ease/very naturally? **Hint: Have a conversation with each person like we learned about in the chapter on empathy. Learn what excites/drives them. Ask for examples of previous work, see what they enjoyed doing, what came easily, and what they struggled with.

Step 3: Use their skills/natural talent where best suited. As you worked backwards from the project's end goal, you should be able to see where each team member fits into the project plan.

Step 4: Remove the obstacles. You being in the leadership role of this team are responsible for shielding them against all the corporate BS. Imagine yourself as a snowplow, and the snow is all the corporate BS.

This will take some time to master. Your first team or two may not be the 95-96 Chicago Bulls. But the more you do this, the better you'll get. Building teams has become one of my favorite things to do. If you were to pull me onto a project, building the team out would be my natural talent. I love helping people find their hidden potential. I've been able to hone in on helping people get more from themselves than they ever thought possible.

One team-building experience I loved was several years back. A teammate approached me with a mission that would have massive impact for our organization.

The mission was to build a Design Language System (DLS). A DLS is a set of rules or guidelines that heightens the level of harmony in a digital ecosystem. It's basically a set of guidelines that tell designers, engineers, and product managers how an app should look, feel, and operate.

The easiest example of a DLS component is a button. A button in an app has multiple states. Default, Hover, Focus, Active, Disabled and Loading/Processing. Each of those states needs a design, color, font, sizing rules, action. What a DLS does is help set that as a standard so that all apps within a certain company or brand look/feel/act the same for the user. Nothing is worse than picking up an app built by the same company and having to learn how it works. The DLS helps maintain consistency and improves user experience.

The company I worked for didn't have a Head of Design or even a team lead for design. Due to my level of followers and the respect I had in the organization, I stepped into this role and built a team to help build the DLS. The team I built wasn't a formal team, they didn't report to me, but were excited to support the mission.

With the end goal being a DLS, I knew I would need designers, engineers, copywriters, someone from the marketing team, and someone from the internal Drupal team. All of these people were joining this project as a secondary effort to their day job. Getting them to join made it extremely important to have a strong Why statement.

As I built the team, I ignored departments and managers and went directly to the individuals that were needed for success. I started off by pitching them on the mission of the project.

To sell someone on your mission (the Why) your pitch needs to be twofold. One, the mission needs to be inspiring. The Why needs to somehow make the world a better place. When I went out and talked to UX/UI Designers, I knew their passion was in UX/UI. So my pitch to them around the mission focused on their own internal Why and how it connected to the Why of the mission.

Second, I needed to help show them that something was in it for them. I gave them confidence that by being part of this team they would see career growth through the impact they would provide. But to also assure them their manager would support their work on this project, so they could focus on providing value without having to be disturbed by a boss wondering what they're doing.

Next, I started to dig for their natural talent. I went one by one through the people that I needed so that I could reassess my list of needed talents each time I brought someone new on-board.

Once I knew their natural talent, I then assigned them to a piece of work. For example, one of the designers was extremely talented in group brainstorming and creativity. So it was his goal to help bring the team together for sessions like that when needed. That was his focus. Other designers had expertise and greatly enjoyed color theory. They then ran point on helping choose colors for certain scenarios.

Everyone came together, completing the team build, allowing us to move onto project development and task assignments. Once that was done, I got out of the way. I let them do their job and I started snowplowing. I blocked them from extra meetings, made sure their managers knew the great value they were providing, helped them avoid less valuable projects, and funded any supplies needed.

Because of my actions, everyone was able to operate at high efficiency. However, when you operate as a diminisher, you get the opposite. Here is what a diminisher would have done in this situation:

Team building consists of people pleasers, or anyone who will "bow to their will." This makes manipulation easy, as the diminisher succeeds in their ideas without any impact, and sadly receives much worse output than if a multiplier's approach was taken.

Anyone who offers any different ideas from the diminisher is openly mocked. This quickly lowers team input and squelches creativity. People who are unhappy are 31% less creative and often only give 25-50% of their potential (24).

As the deemed "special project" fails to meet promised expectations — like promotions and career accelerations — team members decrease output. In fact, many stop working on the project altogether.

Multipliers Create An Intense, Yet Inspiring Workplace

Now that you have your team, you need to keep them motivated to produce at their top level. Again, there is a step-by-step formula to help you achieve this.

Step 1: Give people room to do their job. You hired them and/or asked them to join for a reason.

Step 2: Ask for the team's best work. Tell each member, individually and collectively, that you're excited they're on the team. Confirm they all understand the Why of the project and make sure they understand the importance of doing excellent work for this initiative.

Step 3: Don't punish failure. Tell the team to be experimental. The faster they learn, the better the outcome will be.

Step 4: Ask for feedback. Be open and honest when requesting feedback. Show you are making an effort to make changes for improvement. This doesn't mean you have to agree with all feedback, but you must acknowledge it.

I'm partial to this section on creating an intense and inspiring workplace, because I've excelled at creating teams that deliver amazing value, and I take pride in what they've delivered.

Part of this intense and inspiring workplace was a group activity we did every Friday. It was called "Appreciation Friday." I borrowed the process from Amy Poehler (25). Here is how it went…

- One person starts by showing their appreciation of another person. This could be for help that person gave them on a tough piece of work or for good work they did on a project.

- The person appreciated would then pay it forward to another person.

- This continues until everyone in the group has been appreciated.

- Once someone has been thanked/appreciated, no one can thank/appreciate them again. This helps make sure the process is inclusive.

On my last day of being Head of Product & Engineering, we did this exercise. The team decided to switch things up on me, and instead of going around the circle, everyone in the group took turns showing appreciation towards me.

When it was his turn, one of the Tech Leads (Sr. Engineer on the team) turned to me and said, "I've been struggling with this since I got here. I can't tell if you're lazy or if you just have ultimate trust in me. But man, I've accomplished more in my role with you in the last six months than I did in the last three years at my former company."

He was right. I did have ultimate trust in him. I hired him to do a job and I pushed him, using the steps above to achieve more than he thought possible.

The reason he could say this is because I'd executed well on the four steps: Give people room to do their job, ask for their best work, don't punish failure, and ask for feedback. I snowplowed well, but I also empowered everyone on the team to make decisions. Not only that, but I also *supported* their decisions. They would receive the credit for things that went well, and I would own anything negative that didn't workout.

This gave each person on the team the opportunity to take ownership in a way they hadn't before. It inspired them to want to try out their own ideas when solving a challenge, because they knew failure wouldn't be punished if it didn't work.

Along the way, I had 1x1's with every person that reported to me every other week. Those that didn't report to me I met with 1x a month. Their line managers were expected to do it every other week.

In these 1x1's, I brought no agenda. It was simply their time to connect with me and let me know what was going well and what wasn't. This simple setup was extremely effective because I spent most of our time listening, maybe telling a few jokes.

When someone on your team tells you about a project/task/etc. that's not going well, you have three options you can take:

1. Fix it for them. Figure out the root cause and fix it.

2. Give them guidance on how to fix it for themselves. Empower them to find a solution and try it.

3. Give them guidance on why this issue should be left alone. Share reasoning/personal history/past experience with similar situations. Ask them to let it sit for a few weeks and bring it up again if it's still bothering them.

With number three, you're not ignoring the issue, but tabling it. It shows that you're listening to them and not just ignoring something that is genuinely bothering them.

When going through the steps above, if you are consistently landing on step 3, something is wrong. If this is happening, your team will begin to lose trust in you and most likely your connection to the team is missing.

As a diminisher, you'd probably take a completely different route...

You'd toss your power around as a superior and point out everyone's mistakes.

- You'd make sure to especially point out mistakes in public settings. This will stop others from challenging you and bringing up ideas that weren't yours.

- You'd listen to ideas in private and then steal them as your own.

- Over time, people on the team will try to predict what you want, completely destroying any quality output that your team is able to provide.

Multipliers Challenge And Push A Team

Now that your team is built and you've got an intense and inspiring workplace, you'll need to make sure you keep that intensity alive by continuing to challenge and push the team.

When leading a project or your followers, you'll get the most from them if you challenge them to bring their best self to work every day. A challenging and inspiring workplace is one that people love coming to every day, knowing they'll go home exhausted from a challenging day's work. They tell their significant other or friends all the awesome things they're able to do, because finally they have found a leader they truly can get behind.

Here are the steps to make that happen:

Step 1: Point people in a direction. Don't tell them exactly what needs to be done, just point them in the direction of the final project deliverable. Let them figure out the rest.

Step 2: Help define the challenges.

Step 3: Inspire belief.

Let's go back to the example of the Design Language System. Bringing this team together, explaining the Why behind building a DLS, and selling them on the project's vision completed step one. I pointed them in the direction of a DLS and defined its purpose.

As challenges arise, you need to share them with your team. For example, in building a DLS, you are going to run into obstacles with other design teams at the company. Where your focus is on mobile and web apps, other design teams are designing marketing pages, print media, and social media designs. What you do can affect their work and vice versa.

One challenge of this work was having multiple teams try to stay in sync, to know when their design changes affect ours and our design changes affect them. This challenge is something I kept the team aware of, yet managed myself. This should not trickle down in their day-to day-work and add unnecessary stress, unless you've assigned someone on the team to manage this directly because their natural talent lends well to this scenario.

As you work towards your project/mission, there are going to be ups and downs. Downs may include: missed deadline(s), team members leave the team/company, executives challenging the reason you're doing the work, another team trying to do the same work, or the mission might iterate and you now have a new target.

On the flip side, there are many ups. You hit deadlines and deliver what was expected. People get excited about what you're doing and speak highly of you. You complete pieces of the project and start to have massive impact for the corporation. You or a team member gets promoted for incredible work.

In creating the DLS, we had many downs. We'd randomly lose a person from the team, or marketing would make a play to take over some of the work we were doing. Challenges like that can affect someone's belief in the mission and the worthiness behind what you're trying to accomplish. It's on you to make sure their inspiration stays high, maintaining devotion.

The best way to succeed in this is to work in an Agile way. Remember, it's best to break down large pieces of work into smaller tasks. Look to complete and deliver on these tasks every one to two weeks (A Sprint). By doing this, it makes it easier for you to maintain inspiration within the team.

As you move along, you'll be delivering results each Sprint, which will help keep inspiration and spirits up amongst the team. At each Sprint, team members will have something they can show you, their teammates, and co-workers. This action is powerful because it gives them a constant reminder that they are working towards a larger mission. In each Sprint review and retrospective, you have the opportunity to reiterate this, keeping inspiration high.

Putting This Into Action

- As a multiplier you can get 2x the output from your team.
    - Diminisher: 20-50%
    - Multiplier: 70-100%
- When building a new team, create an action plan that includes the steps above. Check them off as you build out the team.
- If you've got a team, review that you have the right people. Go through the steps as if you were building the team again. If you have the right people, make sure you've maximized their natural talent.
- As a team lead, inspiration and removing obstacles are your top two initiatives. Most of your focus will be placed here.
- Make sure to request the best from your team.

Chapter 10: Don't Be a Micromanager

"You hirec people for a reason. Let them do their job." - Brandon Dohman

This quote pretty much sums up this chapter. If you're constantly looking over someone's shoulder, you're acting in a diminishing capacity. That means you're getting 20-50% of their capability. If you're getting that level of capability from those around you, you're not proving to anyone you should be promoted to a higher level. Remember, the higher up you go in the corporation, the more you need to be managing people instead of worrying about daily tasks.

As we learned earlier, micromanaging usually comes from a place of distrust. This lack of trust isn't always because the person on your team is doing poor work, but it could be from the boundaries you've set for that person. Here are some examples that will help you define a micromanager…

- You're being overly restrictive with those that report to you, requiring your permission to make any project decision.
- You request to be copied on all project emails your team sends.
- You request invites to all project meetings.
- You don't act as a snowplow and make team members handle their own political battles with other managers or directors.
- Constantly request progress reports and proof of daily activities.
- You don't delegate, or if you do, you delegate very few tasks out to your team.
- You don't mentor or work to upskill your team.

As we mentioned in the first chapter on ownership, you need to take a look at the items you have or have not done that could be causing problems. In the case of micromanagement, there is a lot you most likely haven't done that pushes you to want to look over someone's shoulder.

To keep yourself from being a micromanager, there are a few simple steps you can follow:

Step 1: Clearly define the ownership stake your team members have. Make sure everyone knows what they are in charge of and responsible for. Ownership motivates people to produce at their highest work output .

Step 2: Make sure they have resources to get their job done. This could require you having to manage upwards so that your boss provides a budget, or anything that helps your team succeed.

Step 3: Ensure people are held accountable. If someone is responsible for a certain task, make sure the results are up to them. Hold them accountable for those results.

By doing these steps, you can create a very streamlined environment that helps everyone know what their task is, what is expected of them, and that they will be held accountable. That way if something doesn't get done, you can easily identify the gap.

Holding someone accountable doesn't mean that you then berate or are negative towards them for not delivering. That would be a diminishing act. If someone doesn't deliver, go back to what we learned about empathy and dig to find out why.

As you dig, take notes on what you've learned. There is a good chance this will be a teaching moment for the both of you. For you, you'll learn more about how to spot missteps before they happen and take ownership where you could have supported this person better. Don't let ego get in the way here. Don't place blame on someone to protect your status.

For them, it will be a lesson in ownership. Utilize this teaching moment, and guide them in understanding the power of ownership and the three steps necessary for them to help rectify the situation so this doesn't happen again in the future.

One of the less common components of micromanagement that is discussed is the detriment to your own personal time. If you're acting as a micromanager and doing even one of the activities above, you're going to keep yourself from having massive impact. Why? Because you're wasting your entire day following other people around, checking to make sure they get their work done without doing your own.

Micromanaging often leads to half-assing everything, accomplishing nothing that is of real value to the company. So not only are you not producing anything, but your team isn't either. That's a recipe for unemployment.

Anytime you feel the need to look over someone's shoulder, take a step back and look to understand why.

Putting This Into Action

- You hired someone or brought them onto your team for a reason. Let them do their job.

- Follow the steps to make sure you are setting up clear ownership across tasks.

- Make sure people are held accountable for their output.

Chapter 11: How To Have A 1x1

"Your presence is the most precious gift you can give to another human being."

— Marshall B. Rosenberg

I'm going to keep this section short and to the point. This chapter is written from an internal place of anger. Partly anger at myself for getting this so wrong, and partly for managers that I see still get this very wrong.

The purpose of scheduling a 1x1 can vary from time to time, but the ultimate goal is to connect with the other person, to help them feel heard, validated and valued.

Whether they are a direct report, a coworker, or a friend, anything you do other than pay attention to them is disrespectful. Here are some workplace examples of disrespect:

- You check and answer emails while having a 1x1 with one of your reports.

- You check and answer instant messages while having a 1x1 with one of your reports.

- You continue to work while a coworker stops by to talk.

- You scroll through social media while having a conversation with a coworker/teammate.

- You let your mind wander to other thoughts/activities without focusing on what someone is telling you.

I could go on and on with examples, and I'm sure you can think of many more. I get angry and frustrated when I see this and angry at myself when I become aware I'm doing something in the above. Through practice, I've drastically reduced my disrespectfulness in 1x1s.

By doing any of the above items, here is what the person who is there to talk with you is hearing:

Whatever task you are doing is more important than me as a person.

Think about that for a minute. Let that sink in. If you're having a 1x1 conversation with someone and you are constantly distracted, what you are saying to that person, directly or indirectly, is that they are less important than whatever is on your screen.

Here is an example. I had a boss who was in a different location than I was. We did 1x1s every other week over video. During the 1x1s, I saw more of the side of their head than I did them looking at me and having a conversation. There were these weird, awkward pauses when they replied to emails or instant messages. They'd even ask me to repeat what I said at times. We only met for 30 minutes every other week. Outside of that, we never really spoke.

The 1x1 time we had was for me to share and engage with them on things I needed help on, or things that were going well. Oftentimes, we never even got to that because they were "so busy." So eventually I just stopped sharing anything.

To have a good 1x1 or a good conversation with someone, you need to be present. Here are a few quick, easy steps to make sure you can make this happen—

- Put your electronics on silent. Turn the ringer/vibration off on your phone, close your laptop, or go to screensaver mode.
- If you are a manager, be consistent with your 1x1 times and don't reschedule them.
    - Yes, crazy things happen. But if you reschedule over 10% of your 1x1 time slots, you're being disrespectful.
- If the conversation is impromptu and you're not free to talk, tell the person that directly. Ex: Hey, I'm trying to finish this up, can I come find you in 30 minutes?
    - Doing this is more respectful than not listening to them and continuing to work.

And before you say, "Ohh but Brandon, I'm a great multitasker, I can do both."

No. No you can't.

Why? Because science says it's impossible and you are confused on what multitasking really is.

Mult-tasking is listening to a podcast and doing the dishes or walking and chewing gum. Doing work and talking to someone at the same time is multi-concentration, and multi-concentration isn't possible. Our brains cannot focus on two items at once. We can't be fully present or offer our best work in both scenarios.

So if you're talking to someone while still doing work, you're half-assing both items. The conversation won't be valuable, and neither will the work you're doing. Remember, one of the ways to advance in your career is to have massive impact. How can you have massive impact if you're half-assing most of your work?

Putting This Into Action

- Be present when you have a conversation with someone. Ditch the tech, be with them in the moment.

- Listen to others and ask questions that offer a space for openness, honesty, and vulnerability.

- If you struggle with small talk or can't find things to say, switch to mirroring.

Section 3 Checkpoint

Everything you've learned in this book is designed to scale. Meaning, it works on the first day in your career through the day you retire as an SVP or Chief. In Section 1 on Mindset, the teachings were more internal. Section 2 we started to see the value of working smart. Components that could work well for you and a team.

Section 3 is where we see the organizational scale of what you learned. It's about how to build great teams. The mark of true leadership is that ability to build great teams and have them excel. Teams built strongly around a Why, full of people who eagerly come to work each day giving their best to help make the world a better place.

This last section holds the true power to your advancement. It's built upon the previous two sections, but in those previous two sections they were still devoted to helping you with your mindset and how to work smarter. But in this section, we're pushing real change to your organization.

These learnings are extremely powerful. Why? Because "nine out of ten people are willing to earn less money to do more-meaningful work(26)". Think about that for a minute... This study is saying that 90% of workers would take a pay cut to do a job that is more meaningful to them.

Section 3 gives you that ability to make work more meaningful for everyone you encounter. The ability to truly maximize their talent and inspire them to action in a challenging environment, but giving them the confidence that you're there for them ready to help them along the way.

This help is not only something you'll be able to provide to others in their career, but something I aim to help you with as well. My coaching program will challenge and inspire you, pushing you to tackle new challenges. But with that added comfort of knowing someone is there to support you along the way. If you're interested in help along your journey, please submit an application by going to www.dynamiccorporateleader.com/program-application

Putting It All Together

What to do next?

Congratulations! You've made it through the book. I know that I've provided a lot of information above, and you're probably wondering what you should do next. It's simple…

Do something

Far too many people are searching for the perfect combination of tools, practices, and methodologies before they start trying to make their career better. There is no perfect anything, and there never will be. Just get started doing something.

I ran into this problem when I started competing in Strongman. I kept looking for the smartest person, the best coach, the most up to date training methodologies before I would start training a competition. I wanted to make sure I was being efficient and would be able to beat everyone in competition because I was the most knowledgeable person there. I trained better and I did the best workouts.

Over a few months, competitions slipped by, workouts missed, because I was in search of the best way to workout. I made zero progress during this time of research and discovery.

Had I just gone to the gym and done some form of weight lifting (not caring about the what or how), I would have been much stronger than sitting on my butt reading articles about Hafthor Bjornsson and Eddie Hall's training and diet regime.

I don't want to see people who are looking to advance their career continue down the same path, where they continually research, discover, and never implement. Of going back to school and getting another MBA or advanced degree before they feel like the time is right to finally get up and ask for that promotion.

Each day of our life builds upon the one before it. If you don't put yourself in a position to experiment and be agile, you'll be far behind those who do.

Will there be some who still outperform you. Yes. Will you outperform many others? Absolutely. But you can't do that if you don't get started.

Start today. Start taking ownership. Start understanding your coworkers, and get to know them on a personal level. Start engaging in Agile practices. Make tons of mistakes and learn from them. If you don't, you'll continue to be where you are today. And what fun is that?

How To Get More Help

As this book comes to a wrap, you've hopefully been able to fill in some gaps on how to actually succeed and advance in your career. These important concepts and new learnings you've encountered are here to help take you where you want to go. But some of you may be wondering how to utilize these key components in your personal journey. How can I really hone in on my skills at work? How do I take ownership in this situation? Where do I need to shift my mindset? How do I even start implementing these in my work life?

This is where the power of mentorship comes into play. Someone to come alongside you in this journey, to help you achieve your goals (or even speed up the process of achieving your goals). Mentorship is a basic fundamental so often absent in the working world. Relationships are key in unleashing new potential and opportunity, and the journey can be lonely if we walk it alone. That's why I launched my coaching program, an opportunity to work with you 1x1 to help you grow and succeed and tackle any challenging circumstances you're experiencing. In addition to 1x1 office hours, my program offers 60+ video and podcast style trainings, weekly group coaching calls to network with others and learn from their experiences, and a private slack channel to get support outside of office hours.

Disclaimer: This program is for ambitious people who want genuine support and honest feedback in helping them get to where they want to go. I'm supportive and will work hard to make sure you succeed, but this is also a no-bullshit kind of program. I'm not afraid of calling out excuses or poor habits, because my role as a mentor is to accelerate you as you pursue your goals.

As you learn and grow, in all that you do, remember to treat others with respect and kindness. We're all on our own journeys, and it's important we seek to understand the path each one of us is on, no matter how different. It's easy to cast judgment in areas that we don't know or understand, which is why it's critical that we use empathy and open our hearts to others along the way.

If you're interested in mentorship through your journey I'm here to help. To get started fill out an application form at www.dynamiccorporateleader.com/program-application.

Additional Resources

I've included a few extras for you to access as a reader of this work. It's part *thank you* and part *I didn't have enough room in the book, but I want to teach it to you.*

The links below will take you to privately hosted videos where you can access the additional training. These trainings supplement everything you've learned so far in the **Dynamic Corporate Leader Method.** While the book offers a complete way for you to advance your career, as you hone in on the skills taught, you'll find new instances in which you'd like to refine your skills.

I've also included more information that will go over what is offered in the Dynamic Corporate Leader Coaching Program. This short video will discuss in detail the program, group coaching and 1x1 coaching that is available.

How To Get To The Root Of Any Problems Using The 5-Whys Technique

Ever get stumped by a really hard challenge? Or struggle to break down a big challenge (your Think Big) into manageable chunks? The 5-Whys technique is the answer to all your struggles. Using this technique will simplify the process of defining why something happened and help you better design solutions to fix a problem or solve a solution.

5-Whys Exercise

Why You Need To Stop Talking Shit And How It's Ruining Your Career

This video is an enhancement on the mindset section of this book. All too often we find ourselves at work speaking negatively of others. At times it becomes easy/simple to bond with a co-worker over a mutual disdain for others. Your disdain may be something minor, but that something minor can greatly inhibit your career progression.

The Need To Stop Talking Shit

Full Overview of The Dynamic Leader Coaching Program

In joining the Dynamic Corporate Leader Coaching Program, you'll get lifetime access to 60+ video and podcast style trainings, which are broken into seven modules. Each module covers a new topic that builds off the previous, with lessons delivered in a way that allows you to immediately implement the learnings in your career.

We also offer two ways of assistance outside of these lessons: weekly group coaching calls and 1x1 office hours. These provide the opportunity to ask any kind of question, whether that's regarding content or a situation at work. Not only will you get support from me, but also from others who are a part of the program.

Lastly, there is a program slack channel that gives you 24x7 access to support. I promise to respond to every question asked in the slack channel. That way, if you can't make it to office hours, but need the help, you'll quickly be able to receive it.

If you're interested in this kind of support and access to a wide range of resources that'll help you advance your career starting today, submit your application today. Visit www.dynamiccorporateleader.com/program-application to submit your application today!

References

Note: This is a lean list of references. I didn't/don't find it valuable for this effort to properly format them in AMA/MLA style. Apologies to my high school english teachers.

(1) Range: Why Generalists Triumph in a Specialized World

(2) Why Integrity Remains One of the Top Leadership Attributes

(3) Nine Lies About Work: A Freethinking Leader's Guide to the Real World

(4) Are There Universal Facial Expressions?

(5) The Effects of the Micromanagement of Staff on the Business

(6) https://www.google.com/search?q=definition+of+ego (Source: Oxford Languages)

(7) Egonomics: What Makes Ego Our Greatest Asset (or Most Expensive Liability)

(8) Start With Why

(9) Find Your Why

(10) Elon Musk is now the richest person in the world, passing Jeff Bezos

(11) Why Are Thousands Lining Up For The Tesla Model 3?

(12) The Subconscious Mind of the Consumer (And How To Reach It)

(13) Millennials: The Purpose Generation

(14) Impact Of Autocratic Leadership Style On Turnover Management Essay

(15) Why you should work 4 hours a day, according to science

(16) HBR: Why Constraints Are Good for Innovation

(17) That State of Enterprise

(18) What Is Cognitive Dissonance?

(19) The Prosecution's Case Against DNA

(20) Survey Data Shows That Many Companies Are Still Not Truly Agile

(21) Positive Intelligence

(22) Never Split The Difference

(23) Two-Thirds of America Unhappy at Job -65% Choose New Boss Over Pay Raise

(24) Shawn Achor: The happy secret to better work

(25) Amy Poehler started a tradition on "Parks & Rec" that every workplace should try

(26) 9 Out of 10 People Are Willing to Earn Less Money to Do More-Meaningful Work